To Pray
One Way
is to Vote
One Way

THOMAS W. PAXTON

ISBN 978-1-0980-4448-0 (paperback)
ISBN 978-1-0980-4449-7 (digital)

Christian Faith Publishing, Inc.
832 Park Avenue
Meadville, PA 16335
www.christianfaithpublishing.com

Printed in the United States of America

Contents

How happy is the man who does not follow the advice of the wicked or take the path of sinners or join a group of mockers! Instead his delight is in the Lord's instruction, and he meditates on it day and night.

—Psalm 1:1–2 (NASB)

PART 1

Introduction

Caesar, the Representative of Man
Jesus, the Representative of God

While human leadership is indicated and required in the Bible, it is not supposed to usurp the authority of God.

When a person declares Christianity to be his or her faith, the question must be pondered: What makes that individual Christian? Loads of people go to church on Sunday and pray in a particular way to a particular deity. But when church is over, they return to Caesar's world. When election time rolls around, they forget all they learned in church and vote contrary to the teaching of God. Many of these folks truly think they are in harmony with God's word, but they are ignorant of God's teachings. Through this ignorance, they will cast a ballot in support of a candidate who represents the opposite of their own beliefs. In order to vote in accordance with your faith, you need to know what the God of your faith teaches. *and the candidate*

Part 1 of this study deals with the differences between earthly leadership and spiritual leadership. While the state has no business tinkering with the church, the church needs to be involved in the state. It is not the realm of the church to dictate policy; rather, it is the responsibility of the church to teach how to elect our governmental heads.

While the United States may not necessarily be a Christian nation, it is founded on the principle of freedom of faith. It is a land where people are permitted to choose their faith. It is not mandated that Christianity be the official religion of this country. It just happens that throughout US history, the majority of those who selected a faith chose Christianity.

For those who claim Christianity as their own today, they are simply expressing their freedom to choose. When a person asserts Christianity, he or she is adopting its teachings the same as the individual who accepts the prospectus of Islam, Hinduism, or Buddhism.

Part of the Christian package requires the Christian believer to honor and pray for our church heads as well as our secular governing bodies. We are to select leadership in harmony with God. If we pray one way on Sunday but vote another way on Tuesday, what is it that we are taking home from church?

Is it possible for political values and biblical values to blend?

CHAPTER 1

The Kingdom of Caesar and the Kingdom of God—Can They Share One World?

Political issues always will be divisive because politics reflect the thinking of man. No matter how well-intentioned, the plans of man are always flawed because man is not all-knowing. Only one is all-knowing, and he ain't no man.

Matthew 22:15–21 tells a story of the Pharisees's attempt to trap Jesus. Their goal was to put a stop to this crazy Jesus movement by having him arrested. Try as they might, they, of course, failed. How do you outsmart the one who created smart?

> Then the Pharisees went out and laid plans to trap him in his words. They sent their disciples to him along with the Herodians. "Teacher," they said, "we know that you are a man of integrity and that you teach the way of God in accordance with the truth. You aren't swayed by others, because you pay no attention to who they are. Tell us then, what is your opinion? Is it right to pay the imperial tax to Caesar or not?" But Jesus, knowing their evil intent, said, "You hypocrites, why are you trying to trap me? Show me the coin used for paying the tax." They brought him a denarius, and he asked them, "Whose image is this? And whose inscription?" "Caesar's" they replied. Then he said to them, "So give back

to Caesar what is Caesar's and to God what is God's." (Matthew 22:15–21 NIV)

At first glance, one may think Jesus was telling the Pharisees that everything is cool. Caesar has his laws, and God has his. There are two separate codes to live by. But are there two separate codes to live by? A true Christian knows and understands that there is only one code to live by, the code of our Savior Jesus Christ.

> And there is no God apart from me, a righteous God and a savior; there is none but me. (Isaiah 45:21 NIV)

> I am the way, and the truth, and the life; no one comes to the father but through me. (John 14:6 NASB)

In the gospel of John alone, Jesus alludes to his being the only way to salvation no less than twenty-three times. Understanding that Jesus is the only way, and that there is only one Creator, there can only be one code to live by: the code of Jesus.

Since there is only one Creator, it is more than just an assumption that everything came from him. Everything would, of course, include the trees, the water, the minerals, the animals, the laws of physics, and us. Since all things are his, we own nothing. It all belongs to him. Even our very lives are from him. So let's look at Matthew 22:21 (NIV) again: "So give *back* to Caesar what is Caesar's and to God what is God's."

We can't give back to someone something that was never his to give in the first place. Caesar answers to God the same as Tom Paxton, Barrack Obama, Donald Trump, and the Pope.

> For unto us a child is born, Unto us a Son is given;
> And the government will be upon his shoulder.
> And His name will be called Wonderful Counselor,
> Mighty God, Everlasting Father, Prince of Peace.

> Of the increase of His government and peace
> there will be no end, Upon the throne of David
> and over His kingdom, To order it and establish
> it with judgment and justice From that time for-
> ward, even forever. The zeal of the Lord of hosts
> will perform this. (Isaiah 9:6–7 NKJV)

Caesar laid his image on the coin, but God laid his image on the man. Caesar answers to God just like the rest of us. The kingdom of God is the only kingdom that will last forever. We shouldn't be fooled as the Pharisees were. We must understand the difference between earthly kingdoms and God's kingdom. God's kingdom comes first. Earthly leaders must submit to God.

✓ Christians are required to obey the law of the land. This is bib-lical. We are to honor and pray that our leaders will guide us down a righteous path. We are to be obedient to Caesar in his realm until it encroaches God's realm.

Caesar can tell us what the rules of the road are, but God tells us what the rules of marriage are. We can obey Caesar regarding the rules of the road, but the spiritual regulations that God provides are not of Caesar's jurisdiction. We can give obedience to these rules only to God.

When we start allowing Caesar to correct God, we are making Caesar our god. But wait a minute. How many gods are there? The one true God teaches us the one truth. We are to maintain and return our allegiance to the one who had the power to give out truth in the first place. The same truth God gives us is the same truth he gives our leaders.

Now let us return to Matthew 22:16–17 (NIV):

> You aren't swayed by others, because you pay no
> attention to who they are. Tell us then, what is
> your opinion? Is it right to pay the imperial tax
> to Caesar or not?

At first glance, it appears Jesus doesn't give a hoot in howdy town what anybody else thinks. Anyone who has a relationship with the Lord, however, knows better. He isn't swayed because he is the one with all the answers. We can only learn from him. He knows, understands, and loves all of us equally as individuals. He knows how many hairs we have. He knows all our secrets.

Does he pay no attention to who we are? In a convoluted sort of way. He loves us all and came to save us all. We all need him, but he can gain nothing from us. There is nothing we can do for him. There is nothing we can teach him.

When your dog barks, or your cat meows, or your newborn infant cries, you are not going to learn anything from any of them. It is not likely that any one of them is going to inform you of a revised law of thermodynamics. They are not even aware that $1 + 1 = 2$. They can make you aware only that they are hungry, thirsty, or tired. Since you know the last time they ate, drank, or slept, you already expected to hear from them.

So, although you love them, are concerned for them, and will try to comfort them and meet their needs, you are not going to gain any knowledge by listening to them. You love your baby and will do anything for your little bundle of joy, but the little sweetheart can't teach you a single thing.

We are God's little bundle of joy.

> For the foolishness of God is wiser than human wisdom, and the weakness of God is stronger than human strength. (1 Corinthians 1:25 NIV)

Mix the greatest thinkers in the history of mankind with the greatest carpenters, electricians, botanists, geologists, geographers, mathematicians, writers, educators, physicians, aircraft pilots, law-enforcement experts, historians, zoologists, attorneys, biologists, dictators, kings, prime ministers, presidents, and the great Roman statesman Gaius Julius Caesar; give them eternity to create a place for the spirit of one person to spend a single solitary second after death; and they will fail. Caesar can't save us. Only God can provide such a place of everlasting destiny.

Even though Caesar cannot give eternal salvation, he can still allow God to use him. God will do all the saving. If Caesar resists God and chooses to lead his citizens down an ungodly path, he will become a tool of the devil. Those who follow him will do so into eternal damnation.

God, in his all-knowing way, sometimes uses people who don't appear righteous on the outside. But God knows what he is doing, and he doesn't give up trying to reach us. He wants us to accept his gift of salvation. He wants us to believe that Jesus paid our sin debt on the cross and rose again on the third day. He wants us to repent in our hearts and confess with our mouths. When we accept his offer and are immersed in the Spirit, the Spirit will guide us and help us discern the truth of God from the deception of the devil. The devil uses God's own law to lead us astray.

> Now we know that whatever the law says, it says to those who are under the law, so that every mouth may be silenced and the whole world held accountable to God. Therefore no one will be declared righteous in God's sight by the works of the law; rather, through the law we become conscious of our sin. (Romans 3:19–20 NIV)

> I would not have known what sin was had it not been for the law. (Romans 7:7 NIV)

God gave us the laws known as the Ten Commandments to show us our need for him. Since we cannot get into heaven with even one blemish of sin, we need some way to wash away that one sin. Jesus is that way.

> Therefore, there is now no condemnation for those who are in Christ Jesus, because through Christ Jesus the law of the spirit who gives life has set you free from the law of sin and death. For what the law was powerless to do because it

> was weakened by the flesh, God did by sending
> his own son in the likeness of sinful flesh to be
> a sin offering. And so he condemned sin in the
> flesh, in order that the righteous requirement of
> the law might be fully met in us, who do not live
> according to the flesh but according to the spirit.
> (Romans 8:1–4 NIV)

We have all broken every single commandment. It is absolutely impossible to keep any of the commandments. This is our weak flesh. So which of our leaders have been stronger in this area? It's awash! We have no business judging each other, as we all have the same sins to our credit.

> Why do you look at the speck of sawdust in your
> brother's eye and pay no attention to the plank in
> your own eye? (Matthew 7:3 NIV)

Is the person who got divorced better than the person who committed adultery in the heart? Not according to God's word. Is the person who physically murdered worse than the one who murdered in the heart? To us, it may seem the actual murderer is worse, but not according to God's word:

> You have heard that it was said to the people a
> long time ago, "You shall not murder, and any-
> one who murders will be subject to judgment."
> But I tell you that anyone who is angry with a
> brother or sister will be subject to judgment.
> (Matthew 5:21–22 NIV)

God makes the rules, not us.

Is the person who steals a million dollars in diamonds worse than the person who steals a nickel? How about the person who illegally cheats the government out of a hundred bucks by lying on his

TO PRAY ONE WAY IS TO VOTE ONE WAY

or her tax forms? There is no money in heaven; stealing is stealing. Taking a paper clip home from work is stealing.

There are no big lies and little lies. There are just lies. None of us can avoid sinning. We all have sin. None of us are any better than anyone else.

> What shall we conclude then? Do We have any advantage? Not at all! For we have already made the charge that Jews and Gentiles alike are all under the power of sin. As it is written: "There is no one righteous, not even one." (Romans 3:9–10 NIV)

> The Lord does not look at the things people look at. People look at the outward appearance, but the Lord looks at the heart. (1 Samuel 16:7 NIV)

Our leaders, like the rest of us, are to strive for righteousness through faith in Christ's resurrection and discernment through the Holy Spirit. This is spiritual maturity.

> For everyone who partakes only of milk is not accustomed to the word of righteousness, for he is an infant. But solid food is for the mature, *who because of practice have their senses trained to discern good and evil.* (Hebrews 5:13–14 NASB, emphasis mine)

All we need for spiritual growth is found between the covers of our Bible. Romans 1:16–17 sums up this truth in the phrase, "For in the gospel the righteousness of God is revealed":

> For I am not ashamed of the gospel, because it is the power of God that brings salvation to everyone who believes: first to the Jew, then to the Gentile. For in the gospel the righteousness of

15

> God is revealed—a righteousness that is by faith
> from first to last, just as it is written: "The righ-
> teous will live by faith." (Romans 1:16–17 NIV)

Marriage and life are just two of many topics that fall into God's realm. One of the reasons our nation was birthed was a search for religious freedom. When the government starts telling us what we may believe and forcing us to act against our faith, then that government is not only siding against God himself, but making itself God by correcting the one who made the rules.

When a student fails an exam, can that student change his grade by altering the questions afterward? $2 + 2 = 4$. If the student wants the answer to be 5, can he change the question to $2 + 3 = 5$? Of course, the student may not. That would make the student the teacher. The teacher makes the rules in his or her classroom, as God makes the rules in his universe. If the student demands the teacher change the answer, then the student is rejecting the truth in order to formulate his or her own reality. Regardless of what the student wants the answer to be, the answer is still 4, and the question remains $2 + 2=$.

We live in God's classroom; he makes the laws of morality and salvation.

> Woe to those who quarrel with their maker, those
> who are nothing but potsherds among the pot-
> sherds on the ground. *Does the clay say to the pot-
> ter, "What are you making?"* (Isaiah 45:9 NIV)

Every president, from George Washington to Donald Trump, has been unworthy of God's kingdom. All have been sinners incapable of attaining everlasting life with the Lord in heaven unless they have accepted Christ, repented from their hearts, and confessed God's kingdom with their mouths. If those leaders who have passed into eternity truly believed and accepted the gift of salvation while they walked this earth, they are now with the Lord, just like anyone else.

That being said, in the United States we elect a commander in chief as our leader, not a pastor in chief. There are any number of secular issues our governmental leaders must address.

In the world we have made for ourselves through our immersion in sin, a military needs to be maintained. Public services such as electricity, water, gas, parks, schools, as well as police and fire protection, need financial support to operate. Roads, bridges, and rails need maintenance because without rails and roads, farmers can't deliver food. These simple, basic needs are the basis for public taxation. And that is the realm of Caesar.

But what about the needy and the afflicted? Are they in Caesar's domain or God's? While there is certainly nothing wrong with a good and righteous government directing some portion of tax money to aid the unfortunates, this actually falls into God's area and goes all the way back to Leviticus 19:9–10, which is repeated almost verbatim in Leviticus 23:22:

> When you reap the harvest of your land, do not reap the very edges of your field or gather the gleanings of your harvest. Do not go over your vineyard a second time or pick up the grapes that have fallen. Leave them for the poor and the foreigner. I am the Lord your God. (Leviticus 19:9–10 NIV)

Even caring for the needy among God's children (us) is not the government's responsibility. God wants his children to care for their siblings.

> If anyone is poor among your fellow Israelites in any of the towns of the land the Lord your God is giving you, do not be hardhearted or tightfisted toward them. Rather, be openhearted and freely lend them whatever they need. (Deuteronomy15:7–8 NIV)

Our government leaders really have a much easier task than they understand. But instead of letting the Almighty Creator take care of things that are his to take care of, our leaders are insisting they can take care of us better than God can. As expected, they are failing miserably.

Bottom line: Caesar is to fix our streets, keep the water flowing, and protect us from our domestic and international enemies. Everything else is God's responsibility!

Our leaders are just like us. Without a Savior to pay their sin debt, they're going to hell. So what differentiates a righteous leader from an unrighteous leader? It's certainly not their sin or lack of sin. God uses all kinds of people, some of whom will leave you slack-jawed and speechless. Until you begin to recognize the way of God, you will celebrate these people.

To recognize God's way, you need to recognize God. To recognize God, you need to have a relationship with him. To have a relationship with him, you must study his word. Talk to him. Pray and open your mind to discern the truth of God's everlasting love. Ask him to show himself.

As an example of a leader who appears to be less than righteous on the outside, let's briefly look at King David. This is a guy who gawked at beautiful Bathsheba while she was taking a bath. Knowing she was married, he still had a sordid affair with her, which resulted in her pregnancy. Then, to cover up the whole mess, he ordered her husband to be sent out on point in battle, making sure there was nobody to cover his back so he would be killed. Nice guy, this David.

He also killed some really big dude. Poor Goliath? Not really. Goliath was asking for it. Read the story for yourself in 1 and 2 Samuel. In the end, what did God say to David?

> When your days are fulfilled and you rest with your fathers, I will set up your seed after you, who will come from your body, and I will establish His Kingdom. He shall build a house for My name, and I will establish the throne of His Kingdom forever. I will be His Father, and He

shall be My Son. If He commits iniquity, I will chasten Him with the rod of men and with the blows of the sons of men. But My mercy shall not depart from Him, as I took it from Saul, whom I removed before you. And your house and your kingdom shall be established forever before you. Your throne shall be established forever. (2 Samuel 7:12–16 NKJV)

After removing Saul, he made David their king. God testified concerning him: "I have found David son of Jesse, a man after my own heart; he will do everything I want him to do." "From this man's descendants God has brought to Israel the Savior Jesus, as he promised." (Acts 13:22–23 NIV)

Yes, Jesus Christ the Savior of the world came from the same line as an adulterer and murderer. David certainly accomplished some hardcore sinning, but he recognized his sin and truly repented. He understood the error of his ways and accepted the consequences here on earth during his life.

We must never think it's okay to sin because "God will forgive us." If we believe that, then we are not real believers; we are just using this God character to pacify our guilt and justify our continued deviant behavior. The ultimate seed of David would not be a sinner at all.

The righteous leader attempts to follow the code of our Savior. The unrighteous leader follows his own code, the code of Caesar. But they both sin, just like David.

Arise, O Lord,
Do not let Man prevail;
Let the Nations be judged in Your sight. (Psalm 9:19–20 NKJV)

Christians can still sin and understand they are sinning. Because of the Holy Spirit living in them, they will recognize that sin, repent, and try to stop. And they will be righteous in the eyes of God. He knows the flesh is weak even though the spirit is strong.

> Now one of the Pharisees was requesting Him to dine with him, and He entered the Pharisee's house and reclined *at the table*. And there was a woman in the city who was a sinner; and when she learned that He was reclining *at the table* in the Pharisee's house, she brought an alabaster vial of perfume, and standing behind *Him* at His feet, weeping, she began to wet His feet with her tears, and kept wiping them with the hair of her head, and kissing His feet and anointing them with the perfume. Now when the Pharisee who had invited Him saw this, he said to himself, "If this man were a prophet He would know who and what sort of person this woman is who is touching Him, that she is a sinner." (Luke 7:36–39 NASB)

> Then He (Jesus) came and found them sleeping, and said to Peter, "Simon, are you sleeping? Could you not watch one hour? Watch, and pray, lest you enter into temptation. The spirit indeed is willing, but the flesh is weak." (Mark 14:37–38 NKJV)

Even nonbelievers can read the word of God and understand some of it, but only a Spirit-filled believer can grasp the layers of meaning within the Bible. God reveals deeper truths about himself the more we mature in our faith.

The point of all this is the sins of our flesh are different from the sins of our spirit. The sins of our flesh can be forgiven. Once God forgives them, he makes us clean and acceptable before him. The sins of the spirit, on the other hand, are not accepting the truth of the one true God, not accepting the gift provided by the death and resurrection of Jesus, and rejecting the teaching of the Holy Spirit. God does not forgive the sins of the spirit.

> I tell you, whoever publicly acknowledges me before others, the son of Man will also acknowledge before the angels of God. But whoever disowns me before others will be disowned before the angels of God. And everyone who speaks a word against the Son of Man will be forgiven, but anyone who blasphemes against the Holy Spirit will not be forgiven. (Luke12:8–10 NIV)

Rejecting the Holy Spirit is rejecting the teaching, the gift, the offer of salvation. Correcting God is rejecting God. Satan believes in God, so believing in God is not enough. One must be saved in order to discern the truth of the Holy Spirit's teaching. Anyone who is not saved believes the word of God (the teaching of the Spirit) is correctable. Anyone who believes the word is correctable is quite possibly on his or her way to eternity away from God. If that person does not repent and is not with God after he or she dies, that person can only be in one place where he or she won't be complaining about wind chill.

> Whoever is not with me is against me, and whoever does not gather with me scatters. And so I tell you, every kind of sin and slander can be forgiven, but blasphemy against the Spirit will not be forgiven. Anyone who speaks a word against the Son of Man will be forgiven, but anyone who speaks against the Holy Spirit will not be forgiven, either in this age or the age to come. (Matthew 12:30–32 NIV)

So who are these people who are rejecting the truth? They are the same people who surround us in our everyday trials and tribulations. They may be the loved ones we feel the closest to. They are the people we elect to office, who choose to teach the lies of the devil.

People who allow the devil to teach falsehoods are teaching separation from Jesus. There are more of these poor souls around us than we can imagine. This is why we must not fear telling and living the truth to the best of our capabilities.

> Enter through the narrow gate. For wide is the gate and broad is the road that leads to destruction, and many enter through it. But small is the gate and narrow the road that leads to life, and only a few find it. (Matthew 7:13–14 NIV)

> Though seeing, they do not see; though hearing, they do not hear or understand. In them is fulfilled the prophesy of Isaiah: "You will be ever hearing but never understanding; you will be ever seeing but never perceiving." (Matthew 13:13–14 NIV)

So what is to become of those who can't discern the truth because they refuse to take in the word of wisdom and knowledge? Satan will use them to spread the heresy and lead others away from the truth.

> If anyone causes one of these little ones—those who believe in me—to stumble, it would be better for them to have a large millstone hung around their neck and be drowned in the depths of the sea. Woe to the world because of the things that cause people to stumble! Such things must come, but woe to the person through they come! (Matthew 18:6–7 NIV)

People allow themselves to be deceived because the devil has been around a long time and is crafty. He will use every weakness we have to exploit us. He will even twist the truth to the point of being unrecognizable to the biblically uninformed Christian. He will attempt to convince us that homosexual marriage is a part of the truth, since God loves us all so much. And since all sin is forgivable, and homosexual practice is just another sin, gay marriage should be fine. On the surface, this sounds like the most loving and open opinion.

It is true that homosexual practice is just another sin of the flesh, which can be forgiven, in the same manner that heterosexual sin may be pardoned. It is also true that the self-identifying homosexual is a person of value worthy of God's love, and salvation the same way as the heterosexual's. We are all to love and cherish one another as God loves and cherishes us. The fact that we are broken makes this the ultimate challenge.

But gay marriage is fine only in the eyes of the person who does not know the word. That person has accepted human teaching, not God's.

> You shall not lie with a male as with a woman. It is an abomination. Nor shall you mate with any animal, to defile yourself with it. Nor shall any woman stand before an animal to mate with it, it is a perversion. (Leviticus18:22–23 NKJV)

> Then the Lord God made a woman from the rib he had taken out of the man, and he brought her to the man. The man said, "This is now bone of my bones and flesh of my flesh; she shall be called woman, for she was taken out of man." That is why a man leaves his father and mother and is united to his wife, and they become one flesh. (Genesis 2:22–24 NIV)

> "Haven't you read" Jesus replied, "that at the beginning the Creator made them male and female, and said, For this reason a man will leave

his father and mother and be united to his wife, and the two will become one flesh. So they are no longer two, but one flesh. Therefore what God has joined together, let no one separate." (Matthew 19:4–6 NIV)

For this reason a man will leave his father and mother and be united to his wife, and the two will become one flesh. This is a profound mystery—but I am talking about Christ and the church. (Ephesians 5:31–32 NIV)

Do not be deceived: No sexually immoral people, idolaters, adulterers, or anyone practicing homosexuality, no thieves, greedy people, drunkards, verbally abusive people, or swindlers will inherit God's kingdom. And some of you used to be like this. But you were washed, you were sanctified, you were justified in the name of the Lord Jesus Christ and by the Spirit of our God. (1 Corinthians 6:9–11 HCSB)

The body, however, is not meant for sexual immorality but for the Lord, and the Lord for the body. By his power God raised the Lord from the dead, and he will raise us also. Do you not know that your bodies are members of Christ himself? Shall I then take the members of Christ and unite them with a prostitute? Never! Do you not know that one who unites himself with a prostitute is one with her body? For it is said, "The two will become one flesh. But whoever is united with the Lord is one with him in spirit. Flee from sexual immorality. All other sins a person commits are outside the body, but whoever sins sexually, sins against their own body. Do you not know that your bodies are temples of the Holy Spirit, who is in you, whom you have received from God? You are not your own; you were bought at a price. Therefore honor God with your bodies." (1 Corinthians 6:13–20 NIV)

Christ is the bridegroom of the church. The church is the bride of Christ. We are the church. We are the bride.

God's word lists homosexuality, adultery, bestiality, and several others among the violations of marriage. Homosexuality is becoming more acceptable in American society, however, because those who accept it think they have evolved into a new social maturity. The problem with this human evolution theory is that God does not change, nor do his rules. What's next? Moose sex?

Illuminating the White House in a rainbow of homosexuality is a direct attack on God and his bride. This type of thinking says, "We can do whatever we want, and if it upsets God and all these crazy Jesus nuts, that's even better." Yes, this is a full-frontal assault by the devil himself. Those who propose these measures of attack are allowing themselves to be the hands and feet of Satan. A man who has a divorce in his past (probably before his conversion to Christ) can be forgiven. A man who openly defies the word of God, however, is guilty of the unforgivable blasphemy of Luke 12:8–10 and Mark 12:30–32. Remember the millstone?

To get a better handle on the negative effects of a godless leadership, let's use the book of Acts as a metaphor. In order to accomplish this comparison, some background knowledge is necessary.

The book of Acts was written between AD 63 and AD 70. The events depicted occurred from the death of Jesus to the destruction of Jerusalem. The book is among the first sequels. It is the follow-up to the gospel of Luke, not coincidentally authored by Luke. The Bible had sequels perfected well before Hollywood was wet behind the ears.

There were also political parties and other groups with varying powers and influences back in the day, just like today. The Israel of Jesus's day featured a complex melting pot of political affiliations and religious beliefs blending together much like our modern-day group of crazy, mixed-up congressional representatives. Today, our world is comprised of independents, far-left liberals, left-leaning centrists, right-leaning centrists, nonbelieving conservative right-wingers, evangelical conservatives, atheists, false Christians, Jews, Muslims, thirty-two flavors of sexuality, hungry-hungry hippos, and the list goes on. Just about all these groups have their own bunch of paid lobbyists.

Human government is a mockery of common sense, but we do the best we can, given our limitation, which is our constant questioning of God's ability to provide and lead. In his instruction manual (the Bible), he teaches us how to let him lead us. If we would simply follow his counsel, there would only be two flavors of sexuality, one page of tax code, and a bunch of mature believers patiently guiding another bunch of mature believers, as well some less mature believers. We would have the peace of the Holy Spirit residing within us, and this would be reflected in the state of our nation and the world. Our patience would be as endless as our eternal life with the all-loving heavenly Father.

But that is not the case today, and it was not the case two thousand years ago. God came into the world as a man to pay the price of admission to heaven for all of us. His credit card of forgiveness has no limit. Jesus had to die by our hand to accomplish the task, and we were more than willing to accommodate him. It was a bunch of screwed-up religious and political leaders who got the job done. So, as you can see, the results of godless governing leads to death.

God counted on our cooperation in the crucifixion of Jesus, but he does not want us to continue with the eradication of Jesus. Our contemporary leadership can make the same disastrous mistakes the leadership in Jesus's time made, when people nourished godlessness and rallied around heads of state who would consummate these pagan notions.

Today in America, governing bodies at the federal, state, and local levels, as well as religious leaders, are all siding against Jesus. When a priest or pastor waters down the gospel in a politically correct attempt to fill the church, that priest or pastor is rejecting Jesus in the same heinous manner as the religious zealots of Jesus's time. By infusing the beliefs of man into the teaching of God, a politically correct—spiritually incorrect—religious leader is crucifying Jesus again.

A brief synopsis of the leadership from the period of the gospels through the book of Acts is similar to the chaotic bumbling leadership system we have today. The problem I encounter in providing a quick recap of ancient governing bodies is where to start. So I'll just throw a dart at the board and begin where it lands. I'll leave it up to the reader to tabulate the similarities with the illustrious public representation we live with today. I will, however, provide some detailed clues.

Jerusalem was under the political and military jurisdiction of the Roman Empire. In New Testament times, the great metropolis of Rome was home to a million people. It was the capital of the empire and the seat of Roman power.

In its earlier days as a republic, it was a successful display of early democracy with the people represented by magistrates known as tribunes, who had the power to veto laws and prevent unjust decisions against the common people, known as the plebeians. The people voted in consuls, who held office for one year. The senate advised the consuls, and these senators held office for life. The senators were sort of an advisory committee to the consuls. The patricians were those of noble birth who would dominate the common folk or the plebeians whenever they had the opportunity. This occasional tyranny gave birth to the tribunes. There were other subdivisions of leadership as well, most of which were pseudosafeguards against corruption and misuse of power.

Over time, this experiment in democracy devolved into an empire through a series of assassinations, wars, back-room deals, and power grabs. The senate survived; however, by the time of Christ, it existed as a false demonstration of the freedom of the people. The emperor was considered a practical God, and in some instances, a senator who voiced strong opposition to the emperor risked life and limb.

Any country conquered by Rome became a province governed by a Roman representative. In some cases, the Roman senate controlled the conquered country. These were locals, known as senatorial provinces of Rome, who succumbed to their new authority figures with little threat of violence. When New Testament authors refer to "proconsuls," they are referring to leaders of senatorial provinces.

Other places were considered to be a greater threat to the empire and were controlled by a strong military presence. These provinces were called imperial provinces, as they were ruled by the Roman military, which was under the command of the emperor. A New Testament writer who refers to a "governor" is speaking of the commander of an imperial province. An imperial province means Roman troops are at hand to repress a potential uprising from a people opposed to the presence of Rome. All provinces were heavily taxed for the benefit of the empire.

We know from Acts 13 that during Paul's first missionary journey, Antioch was a senatorial province. Line 7 tells us that Proconsul Sergius Paulus wished to hear the teaching of God from Paul and Barnabas.

Paul's second trip tells us that Corinth was also a senatorial province. Acts 18 tells of the efforts of Paul's enemies to use Proconsul Gallio to eliminate Paul and his Christian teaching. Acts 18:12 identifies Gallio as Proconsul of Achaia (Greece).

When the military conquered Jerusalem in 64 BC, it was Pompey who led the Roman legions into town. At this point, Jerusalem became a province of Rome.

> Early in the morning, all the chief priests and
> the elders of the people made their plans how to
> have Jesus executed. So they bound him, led him
> away and handed him over to Pilate the governor.
> (Matthew 27:1–2 NIV)

Since Pontius Pilate was a governor, we understand the heavy military presence in Jerusalem at the time of Jesus. It was an area of potential revolt. On the surface, it is obvious why Rome felt a certain insecurity about a maintained peace in the region. The Jews' strong belief in their God differed from the Roman belief in their gods. The Jewish people found it greatly offensive that the occupying forces of the empire would bring their standards bearing the image of Caesar to the temple and demand loyalty.

But there was something of a more clandestine nature going on at the same time. Jesus, the Savior of all mankind, was in the world. Satan had gathered all his legions of fallen angels and aligned them in battle formation. The epic struggle of the end-times had begun. The war between good and evil was launching into the final phase of desperation on the part of the devil and was raging in the spiritual world as well as in the physical world. With the arrival of the Messiah, Satan understood that his days were numbered.

Is it any wonder that Roman troops were present? The Jews, who disdained the idea of a false idol taking residence in the temple, teamed up with the idolaters to take on the Savior. If that wasn't a sign of the devil's activity, what was it? The kingdom of God cannot be encroached. The kingdom of Caesar is the kingdom of the world, which is the kingdom of Satan. There is no room for a phony kingdom in the heart of a Christian. A Christian who prays one way is obligated by obedience to live that way, and that includes praying for and participating in the insertion of righteous leaders in the church and the nation. But this obligation to obedience should be desired and come from the heart. If it does not, it is a work of show and means nothing.

The presence of Roman authority in Jerusalem was a nearness of worldly manner. While the Romans were the true outsiders, the devil used them to try to divide and conquer the true believers of God. It was the Romans whom Satan employed to bind together his entire plan of subterfuge.

The Jews had their own hierarchy of leadership. The Sanhedrin came about during the time of Moses. During the forty years of wandering, Moses was the answer man. The people went to him with their questions and worries, and he relayed them to the Lord. Eventually, Moses became a bit overwhelmed and asked God for help. God knows all our limitations, and he had the answers.

> The Lord said to Moses: "Bring me seventy of Israel's elders who are known to you as leaders

and officials among the people. Have them come to the tent of meeting, that they may stand there with you. I will come down and speak with you there, and I will take some of the power of the Spirit that is on you and put it on them. They will share the burden of the people with you so you will not have to carry it alone." (Numbers 11:16–17 NIV)

The Sanhedrin was the supreme court of Jerusalem. It consisted of seventy elders plus one, Moses. As Moses was gone by Jesus's time, the Sanhedrin was seventy-one of what could be described as the cream of the crop: older men of experience, chief priests, scribes, and the most learned men in Jewish law. The top dog, the Moses replica, was one of even higher esteem, worthy of comparison to Moses.

The Sanhedrin was much like the supreme court of the United States today. It could be dominated by a group more conservative or a group more liberal. As it happened in Jesus's day, the Sanhedrin was top-heavy with Pharisees. Lesser numbers came from the Sadducees, Essenes, and Scribes.

The Pharisees were a group of learned religious men who not only strictly adhered to the written law from Sinai but also strongly believed in the verbal law handed down from Moses. They were not worshiping Moses. Rather, they understood that the Lord spoke through him, and they chose to obey the teachings as if they came from the lips of God to their ears. Since God selected Moses for this purpose, the Pharisees got it right.

In the early years, the Pharisees were a true God-honoring outfit. They taught what the Lord told. Unfortunately for them, they degenerated to a mere self-pontificating religious group. Many of them prayed with many words, out in the open to impress the people with their piousness. These prayers were not for the glory of God but for the glory of themselves. As long as the public believed they were more faithful and knowledgeable than the commoner, the Pharisees could maintain control over the people.

The Pharisees desired to maintain authority over the masses. Sounds an awful lot like our politicians today. They may have lived a couple thousand years ago, but they were still human. It is all of humanity's sin nature that corrupts us. The Pharisees believed in a messiah, in the resurrection, and in an eternal afterlife. The roots of the group were based in biblical truth, but they managed to screw it up with the need for self-gratification through personal power.

Another Jewish religious group active in Jesus's time was the Sadducees. The primary difference between the Sadducees and the Pharisees was that the Sadducees only accepted the written word and put much less credence in the verbal traditions of Moses. Although it is not absolute, many believe the Sadducees didn't subscribe to the idea of the resurrection and an eternal life. The Sadducees drew most of their support from the aristocracy, and most were members of the wealthy ruling class.

It is plain to see that these two groups could get into some pretty intense arguments, which meant that control of the Sanhedrin was a vital concern to both sides.

Yet, another group to vie for control of the Sanhedrin were the scribes. A scribe was a highly educated master of detail. The scribes were primarily a political group and experts in the law of Moses. The initial duty of a scribe was to expertly and flawlessly copy the Pentateuch (the five books of Moses, from Genesis to Deuteronomy). Soon they became interpreters of God's law. Dominated by their rigid following of the rules of law, however, they missed the point behind the law and were criticized by Jesus. Like the Pharisees, the scribes became all outward show of knowledge with no inward realization of the truth.

> Then Jesus spoke to the crowds and to his disci-
> ples, saying: "The scribes and the Pharisees have
> seated themselves in the chair of Moses; therefore
> all that they tell you, do and observe, but do not
> do according to their deeds; for they say things
> and do not do them. (Matthew 23:1–3 NASB)

The scribes and Pharisees were most similar in one respect: Jesus put them down in equal amounts.

> Woe to you, scribes and Pharisees, hypocrites! For you clean the outside of the cup and of the dish, but inside they are full of robbery and self-indulgence. You blind Pharisee, first clean the inside of the cup and of the dish, so that the outside of it may become clean also. Woe to you, scribes and Pharisees, hypocrites! For you are like whitewashed tombs which on the outside appear beautiful, but on the inside are filled with dead men's bones and all uncleanness. So you, too, outwardly appear righteous to men, but inwardly you are full of hypocrisy and lawlessness. (Matthew 23:25–28 NASB)

No different than today, in Jesus's time, a multitude of organizations were searching for solutions to problems using a variety of methods.

The Zealots were more of a militaristic bunch of resisters to Roman authority. They adamantly opposed paying the Roman taxes and led violent uprisings.

The Dead Sea Scrolls were not only a great discovery of Old Testament documents written about one hundred years before the birth of Christ, but they were also a modern enlightenment of a group called the Essenes, a scribe-like assemblage operating out of Qumran within a strict observance of the law. Like the scribes, the Essenes were expert copiers. They didn't miss a thing and dotted all the Is. They kept and physically recreated the scriptures with an expert eye. There was no room for a mistake when preserving God's word.

Their observance of the law was as flawless as their copying; however, they were self-segregated groups, believing they had an understanding of scripture that others did not possess. They believed the Old Testament prophecies were going to happen in their time and felt superior to other people, so they sealed themselves off from society.

The Herodians were more of a secular organization interested in preserving some semblance of Israeli national identity. They felt it wise to submit to Roman rule in exchange for some self-governing authority. The Herodians also teamed up with the Pharisees to eliminate Jesus.

So there were a lot of groups with a lot of agendas. They had one big thing in common however: they shared a unanimity in disposing of Jesus.

The politics of then are synonymous with the politics of today. The Herodians are synonymous with liberal patriots. (Let's put America first, but all this God stuff isn't really necessary.) The Zealots are synonymous with conservative patriots. (Just let me keep my guns, and I don't need God. I'll handle things myself.) The Essenes are synonymous with ultraconservative Christians. (Keep away from me, you stinkin' sinners. I'm saved. I'm better than you.) The Pharisees are synonymous with mainstream Democrats and Republicans. In the early days of the nation, both Democrats and Republicans were mostly God-fearing folks who understood the blessings that would be bestowed upon an obedient, God-trusting people. Over time, however, these political parties became corrupt with self-serving attitudes, exactly like the Pharisees.

Human influence started dictating false teaching in the ancient political world as it is doing today. The Jewish commoner did not easily detect this false teaching, just as those who do not know the truth of scripture today would find false teachings difficult to detect.

The political climate today is deteriorating to godlessness in the same manner as it did during Jesus's physical stay upon the earth. One party in particular has gone so far astray that it has publicly denounced believers in God as being stumbling blocks in the path of the nation's need to progress. This party professes multiple anti-God stances as part of its platform of national and international reform.

Over the past twenty-five years, the Democratic Party has adopted to its national platform a full abortion policy with no questions asked of any age girl. During her 2016 presidential campaign,

Hillary Clinton announced her desire to see full-term partial-birth abortions.

Barack Obama celebrated homosexual marriage by illuminating the White House in a rainbow of color. In God's biblical list of violations of marriage, same sex marriage is clearly stated. If you claim to be Christian, yet you believe Barack Obama over Jesus Christ, perhaps you need to reassess your faith.

The same must be said regarding other Democratic Party members choosing their own wisdom over that of God on a variety of issues. Democrats who openly endorse abortion as well as an assortment of other issues that contradict the teachings of the Bible include Bill and Hillary Clinton, Al Gore, Tim Kaine, Chuck Schumer, Nancy Pelosi, and Bernie Sanders. While this is only a tiny list, it is a sample of the thinking of the greater Democratic majority.

While not to the degree of the opposition, the Republicans have hosted their own little godless tendencies, and this is clear evidence of all human corruption. Our political parties are not necessarily to blame, however. The blame falls on the weakness of all humanity. Satan is just good at looking for and finding the little things to exploit in order to divide us. When we fight each other, our sentiments veer from God. When a nation officially condemns the word of God, that nation has little hope of finding the right path until the people of that nation come to their senses and return to righteousness.

The full title of the case that gave a woman the right to abort her baby was *Jane Roe, Et al. v. Henry Wade, District Attorney of Dallas County.* On January 22, 1973, United States Supreme Court judges voted 7–2 that it was a violation of a woman's right to privacy to prevent her from aborting her baby.[1]

By the same twisted logic, one could argue that murder committed on private property should be permissible. Why? Consider the following:

- Real estate surveyors assure the exact boundaries of a person's private property.
- Most police departments are prevented from writing parking citations on private property.

- Peeping toms can be arrested for invasion of privacy.
- Trespassing on private property is not legal.
- Recordings of private conversations are generally inadmissible in a court of law unless a judge deems them warranted before the trial.
- Unwanted noise emanating from a neighbor is considered a violation of the peace, as it is an invasion of the receiver's right to private peace and quiet.

What occurs on the privacy of one's own property is nobody else's business. Since unborn people may be terminated, we must ask the question: "Are my actions anyone else's concern? After all, I have my privacy, especially inside my private body and on my private property!"

If it is okay for a woman to kill her unborn child because the child lives inside her body, and what she does with her body is her private business, then shouldn't anyone have the right to lure somebody into the privacy of their own home in order to murder the person since what occurs is nobody's business?

If this seems absurd to you, it should. Privacy is not justification for murder, regardless of the victim's age. Doesn't the child have his or her own body separate from the mother?

The case of *Roe V. Wade* got the big red ball of abortion rolling in the United States, but it was President William Jefferson Clinton who opened the floodgates of mass murder. On May 26, 1994, he signed into law the FACE Act, which effectively prevented even the suggestion of interference with the act of abortion. The FACE Act, fully titled, is "The Freedom of Access to Clinic Entrances Act of 1994." This act made it a federal crime to interfere with the operation of an abortion center or to attempt to notify patrons of an abortion facility of other options.

While some protections to religious institutions were tacked on to the end of the law, they were an obvious afterthought added to pacify prolife voters. The guts and lifeblood of the FACE Act was to allow for the protection and spread of the prochoice movement.

President Clinton was not done:

- He reversed prior decisions that prevented abortion on military bases.[2]
- He vetoed the partial birth abortion ban.[3]
- He supported the use of the abortion pill, RU 486.[4]
- He reversed American policy that had limited American tax dollars from supporting overseas organizations that used abortion as a means of population control.[5]
- He also signed into law the "National Institutes of Health Revitalization Act of 1993," which, for the first time in American history, allowed public funding for experiments using the tissue (flesh and organs) of aborted babies.[6]

Douglas Johnson, the Legislative Director of the National Right to Life Committee in 1993, said, "Clinton's actions mean that U.S. tax dollars will be used to pressure African and other Third World governments to accept abortion as a method of birth control, although abortion violates the legal, cultural, and religious values of less-developed nations."

Bill Clinton was a Southern Baptist! What we call ourselves means nothing. We can claim membership in any church, but membership in the one church that counts is all that matters. When we join that church, we step into the light of truth and knowledge.

Did Mr. Clinton read the word of God and reject it? Or did he fail to gain the knowledge that should have properly influenced him due to a lack of interest in maturing in his faith? It doesn't make a bit of difference. President Clinton led our nation down the path of evil.

> Do not set foot on the path of the wicked or walk
> in the way of evil doers. (Proverbs 4:14 NIV)

How many Southern Baptists voted for Mr. Clinton because he was a Southern Baptist? What was the thinking of those well-meaning Southern Baptists and members of other earthly denominations who lent support to the Clinton campaign?

The logic could have been that since he was running for president of the United States of America, he must be well-read and thoroughly versed and immersed in his Christianity. Well, as it turns out, he was either not well-read on certain biblical topics or he was versed and immersed in himself.

But how could a true Christian so misunderstand the teachings of Jesus that he would be prepared to correct the teacher?

Bill Clinton is a human being no different than the human beings who elected him. It was those who placed him in office who deserve the lion's share of responsibility for the downward spiral of America's value system that accelerated during his administration. It is the people who put in power a biblically uninformed leader. And they did it through their own ignorance of the truth of God's instruction. We the people gave him the authority to attribute the will of man over the will of God.

Manmade organizations can refer to themselves any way they wish: Southern Baptist, Northern Baptist, Western Baptist, Eastern Baptist, Lutheran, Catholic, Yankees, Giants, Dodgers, Packers, etc. They might be churches, baseball teams, or football teams, but they are noble only in their own eyes. There is only one church, and we can either join it or reject it. Nobody else can make that decision for us. Each of us needs to study, pray about, and discern the truth. When enough of us fail to do this, we become a conglomerate of ignorant fools dangling over the pit of hell. This is precisely when we start creating our own rules of government at the expense of God.

According to the gospel of Matthew, Jesus taught of the final judgment in terms anyone can understand. He said all the nations would be gathered in front of him, the people separated, some going to his right and others to his left.

> Then the King will say to those on his right, "Come, you who are blessed by my father; take your inheritance, the kingdom prepared for you since the creation of the world. For I was hungry and you gave me something to eat, I was thirsty and you gave me something to drink, I was a

stranger and you invited me in, I needed clothes
and you clothed me, I was sick and you looked
after me, I was in prison and you came to visit
me." (Matthew 25:34–36 NIV)

Jesus continued, stating that those righteous souls would ask
him when they did these things.

Truly I tell you, when whatever you did for one
of the least of these brothers and sisters of mine,
you did for me. (Matthew 25:40 NIV)

It will not be the actions of the righteous that will give them eternity with the Lord. The actions will be the end result of accepting the
gift of grace from God, through repentance of sin and understanding
the only way to salvation comes from the sacrifice of the Son. No
good deed can save us. Only the resurrection of Jesus defeated death
and can save us, and we have no method of recreating that through
our pathetic efforts to look good in God's eyes. Our good deeds will
be the result of our desire to please the Lord, and they will be authentic reflections of righteousness automatically inspired by the Holy
Spirit living inside us.

It is this same automatic inspiration from the Holy Spirit that
guides true believers in all our affairs in life, including selecting righteous leadership. We as followers of Jesus must obey God and not
give into sin pressures applied by a godless world. Sin has run amok
in our world and is a sign of the presence of the devil, whose goal is
our destruction. When we let sin destroy us, we bring eternal corruption on ourselves and can only follow and support evil.

Those who think they are voting for a candidate God would
approve of without consulting God's own instruction book will
probably be led by Satan to vote for the candidate most useful to
his evil ways. At this point, such folks are no longer individuals but
commoners betrayed by pride and destined to eternity in the furnace
with the one they really voted for.

To listen to a sermon on Sunday is just not enough. We must remember that the pastor, priest, or other seminary-instructed orator is a human being fully susceptible to Satan's deception. We absolutely must read the word for ourselves to be certain we are on the right path and to be sure of the righteous teachings of our local church heads.

Is the media capable of properly informing us which candidate is the right choice? Let me put it this way: if the teaching of our church leaders must be scrutinized, does it make any sense to believe the talking heads on the boob tube? The vast majority of so-called journalists have as much knowledge of the Bible as I have of the inner workings of the social structure of termites. I suppose somebody has published a book providing the facts of termite society, and I am sure there are people who would love to gain an advanced knowledge of termites, but I am not one of them.

I know nothing of termites, just as most news people know nothing of the Bible. To confirm this as fact, pick a channel, any channel, and listen to the rhetoric. What you will hear is an endless babble of godlessness. If a guest happens to provide a biblical view of any topic, the chatter will turn from simple godlessness to near-violent attacks and threats. The Bible supporter will be accused of hate crimes and compared to Hitler or Stalin, two of the most ardent anti-Semitics and Christian-haters on record. So how could anyone compare us to them? If Stalin was the trap and the believer was the mouse, how could the mouse now be accused of being the trap? It makes no sense to compare those who believe in biblical values to those who persecuted the holder of the same biblical values.

Those who are guilty of comparing Christians to known anti-Christs need to look in the mirror. They are persecuting the Christians physically or with words in the exact same way as Christian-haters of the past. These people are probably frightened to look in the mirror because they might just see a tiny mustache above the lips, so they attack the believers to make themselves less guilty.

It is up to believers to take the hit and demonstrate the faith. God, our Father in heaven, is counting on us to provide the truth to unbelievers. Those unbelievers are us before we accepted the truth, and if those doubters come to believe, we will have new siblings in Christ. So pray for the believing political candidate as well as the unbelieving candidate, but educate yourself in the word of God so you know which one will allow you to spread God's word without restriction.

Can Caesar and God share one world? The question is moot. Since God created Caesar, Caesar is under the dominion of his Creator just like anyone else. God gave us all free will to choose him or not. Should Caesar choose God, we should support Caesar. If Caesar rejects God, we are to reject Caesar. Who shares this world means nothing. Our primary focus should be to share in God's kingdom when we leave this world.

Are you a true Christian? Are you born of Christ and a follower of Jesus? One way to tell is by examining to whom and to what you subscribe. Whose leadership guides you? Perhaps you feel confident in your own leadership. You can be a Democrat, a Republican, or a Libertarian and still be a follower of Jesus, but first you need to know and understand to whom and to what Jesus subscribes.

While the proper use of tax dollars and the condition of roads and bridges are certainly discussions at election time, the most divisive issues are those of a social nature. Friends and families are breaking up over issues they almost never discuss with open minds in the mainstream of life. They bandy opinions about with little desire to self-inform on whichever subject they are discussing. A true Christian should wish to be properly informed on social issues to properly defend the selection of leaders who promote similar values.

The notion that one can vote biblically without understanding the Bible is absurd. Voting habits can be an indication of eternal destiny. Anyone can have a change of heart on a single topic, but when a person makes a 180-degree turn on a slew of issues at the same time, this is an indication of some new information he or she has received. What new info could be so powerful that it alters someone's entire life?

Any true believer in Jesus would certainly want to be educated about what he taught. There is only one source, and no, it is not this book. It is the Bible. To learn of Socrates, read his words. To learn

George Washington's beliefs, read his words. To learn Jesus's teachings, read his words.

Reading the Bible provides something that the words of all other books don't. I'm not talking about the obvious. When one studies Socrates, only the teaching of Socrates is learned. The same applies to any other scholarly work. Only the Bible provides the teaching of more than one person.

Reading the Bible teaches the lessons of God, but it also teaches Satan's methods and philosophy in their entirety. So before we delve into the teachings of Jesus, it is important to understand something of the ways of Satan. Since we align with the devil prior to being born of the Holy Spirit, born-again readers might benefit from being reminded where we came from.

Remember those days of living in darkness and falling to the temptations of the devil? Can you recall the time when your pride allowed the devil to seduce you, when you didn't give a blot about the word of God or the word of Satan? Back in those days, you didn't even realize the devil and his demons were battling God and his angels for your eternal soul. You didn't know it, and you didn't care. You may not have cared, but Satan and God did.

When you stepped into the voting booth, you selected the candidate you thought was best for you, and you were proud of your selection because you knew more than anyone else. Nobody could teach you anything. Without even realizing it, you were practicing a lesson of the devil taught in the word of God. No, God was not praising the devil's way. God was and is trying to warn you of the devil's tactics. This is why Jesus tells of the true existence of hell as well as heaven. He wants us to understand the consequences of succumbing to Satan's deception, and He wants us to be educated about the devil's tactics.

When we cast an election ballot with the understanding that we are more knowledgeable than most anybody else, we are living out the devil's wish. It is our pride that Satan uses to control us.

The word of God tells us whether Caesar and God can share one world. Only the Bible teaches both God's will and Satan's will. These opposing views are revealed in the social issues not only of our day, but of any day. Before looking at the biblical view of some of the most hotly debated issues, it is vital to know the how Satan blinds us to these biblical views.

It is our pride that tells us we don't need to consult the Bible. It is our pride that makes Satan's job so easy.

CHAPTER 2

Pride: The Devil's Attachment to All His Tools

Why do people allow the devil to use them? Most people in their right minds would rather not allow this to happen, but we all have weak areas, and Satan is always looking for them. Once he has uncovered a vulnerable area in our character, he will use every means available to exploit it. Satan is the master craftsman of lies. He is the ultimate deceiver. He is capable of mixing just enough truth with his lies to blend a cocktail designed just for that particular victim, who will then reject his Savior and choose an eternity away from the Lord.

One may wonder why the devil is so into his work. It's quite simple. Satan hates God. Satan doesn't really care all that much about us one way or the other, but he hates God with everything he has. By stealing God's children, he hurts God the Father. It is the only way he can hurt God. Satan is constantly in attack mode. He never stops trying to grab us away from our Father. But Satan can't really take us anywhere. We must make the decision to reject God, which is the unforgivable blasphemy spoken of in Matthew 12:30–32, Mark 3:29, and Luke 12:8–10. The million-dollar question is how do we defend ourselves from the assaults of the devil?

> God resists the proud, but gives grace to the humble. Therefore, submit to God. But resist the Devil, and he will flee from you. Draw near to God, and he will draw near to you. Cleanse your hands, sinners, and purify your hearts, double minded people! (James 4:6–8 HCSB)

God resists the proud because the proud resist God. The proud are those who will not change from their old habits of sin. They are not willing to soften their hearts to accept the change that would be required by accepting the Lord.

When a person has defended a certain idea or principle, that idea or principle becomes embedded in the person's character. The person actually builds this belief into part of who he or she is. After getting opportunities to openly defend this idea or principle, others recognize the thoughts as part of who this person is. Now the person must stick to these thoughts. If the person should reject this idea or principle, then he or she is in effect rejecting himself or herself.

Proud people are elated over their own accomplishments. The proud get satisfaction from the praise of others. When their own ideas or achievements are accepted by others, they feel a sense of gratification. In their minds, they have succeeded. As the proud acquire more personal possessions, they feel growth and respect are occurring.

But is any growth actually happening? Do others have more respect for those who have more physical belongings? The answer is within ourselves. Do you have more respect for someone who has a bigger house, a nicer car, or more money in the bank? No, you don't have more respect for this wealthy person. You may be confusing respect with jealousy. The same is applied to the person whose ideas are accepted by others while your own thoughts or ideas are left to vanquish in your own mind. Do you respect this other person whose thoughts are accepted by others?

If we are honest with ourselves, we can admit that we feel jealously in this area as well. After all, aren't our ideas better than that other person's? If jealousy is a weak point in your character, the devil will use it as a way to bring you away from the truth of God, but the sin topic we are currently discussing is pride.

How can Satan use pride in a person's own accomplishments to lead him or her away from God? The answer is within the word *own*! What we accomplish on our own is usually not what God wanted to accomplish through us. Only when we have the Holy Spirit within us can we do what the Lord wants. Our own accomplishments are invariably sin-natured.

TO PRAY ONE WAY IS TO VOTE ONE WAY

Those who believe people are generally good are either ignorant of the word of God or rejecting it. The Lord looks down from heaven on all mankind to see if there are any who understand, any who seek God.

> All have turned away, all have become corrupt, there is no one who does good, not even one. (Psalm 14:2–3 NIV)

> There is no one righteous, not even one; there is no one who understands; there is no one who seeks God. All have turned away, they have together become worthless; there is no one who does good, not even one. (Romans 3:11–12 NIV)

> Surely I was sinful at birth, sinful from the time my mother conceived me. (Psalm 51:5 NIV)

> The Lord saw how great the wickedness of the human race had become on the earth, and that every inclination of the thoughts of the human heart was only evil all the time. (Genesis 6:5 NIV)

All of us, saved or not, can attest to the words of Jesus in the Gospel of Matthew.

> But the things that come out of a person's mouth come from the heart, and these defile them. For out of the heart come evil thoughts—murder, adultery, sexual immorality, theft, false testimony, slander. These are what defile a person. (Matthew 15:18–20 NIV)

> The heart is deceitful above all things and beyond cure. Who can understand it? "I the LORD search the heart and examine the mind, to reward each

45

person according to their conduct, according to
what their deeds deserve." (Jeremiah 17:9–10
NIV)

As previously stated, even sin in the mind is sin. Temptation to
sin is not sin. Temptation to sin is simply the evil one trying to get us
to sin. When we act out the transgression, we activate the sin (anger,
lust, etc.). But remember that transgressing in our minds is acting
out the sin.

So we have all sinned, and we will all be judged. God doesn't
only remember the good things we have done. The evil is also there,
and it's not going away by itself. The good things we have done will
not wash away the bad. Even if they could, that bad outnumbers the
good by a thousand and ten thousand times.

When we listen to the devil, we can become quite proud of our
own accomplishments. God will see all these wonderful actions we
have taken, and he will forget about our evil nature. When we listen
to the devil, we are all basically good. To believe this is to reject the
word of God as represented in the previously quoted scripture, which
is only a sampling from the full word of God.

Once Satan has our pride convincing us, then we are convicting
ourselves by thinking we no longer need a Savior. Once Satan has
tricked us, our pride will sentence us. Only when every last sin is
washed away and forgotten can we spend eternity with the Father in
heaven. Once we decide we can direct our own destiny, the devil has
won.

This is how sneaky Satan is. He will have us doing all sorts of
nice things until he has us convinced that we don't need a Savior.
We will be so proud of our actions, and that pride will be our doom.
Once we have convicted ourselves with pride, we will begin to make
other prideful, worldly decisions that contradict the teachings of
God because we have subliminally decided we don't need God. Since
we don't need God, we don't need his teachings. We don't need guidance. We can do good things on our own because we know better;
we know what's right. We begin to make declarations by our own

authority. Goodbye, Bible. And the deception is complete. The devil's fruit grows.

> There is a way that appears to be right, but in the end it leads to death. (Proverbs 16:25 NIV)

It may appear right to allow any behavior, but is this not allowing people to be free to live as they wish? Is it not the right of each of us to choose which lifestyle we feel comfortable living?

Some people choose to smoke tobacco, while others choose to smoke a more mind-altering weed. Others choose not to smoke. Some people choose to drink beer, while others select more potent alcohol. Some choose not to drink alcoholic beverages. Some people choose domestic automobiles, while others prefer imported makes.

Some of these choices can indeed be harmful to our bodies. So should we make a conscious decision to harm our bodies? Most people would agree that we should probably choose not to harm ourselves. Any kind of smoking can certainly be destructive to one's health. Yet, the same political wing that disdains smoking cigarettes promotes smoking marijuana. Why is the same attack on tobacco not being made on pot? When people start making decisions on subjects outside their realm of knowledge, they succeed only at making things worse. Again, we see the devil's influence. The same people who claim open-mindedness to any choice reduce the cigarette smoker to second-class-citizen status. Although the true Christian agrees that smoking is unhealthy, the believer does not disdain the smoker as a hated enemy. The Christian understands that the smoker is sinning by damaging God's creation.

Even though a belief in the teachings of the Bible may help the person to quit, the smoker may still not succeed at quitting the habit, but the power of the Holy Spirit will aid the effort he or she is making. If the person fails, at least he or she will understand why he or she needs to quit. The person's Christian family will still love and support him or her and not deride the loved one as someone unworthy of their concern. This physical sin is not the all-condemning sin of the Spirit.

In the Old Testament, God's sanctuary was within the Holy Place in the temple, accessible only by the holiest of priests. Today all of us can have direct access to God. Anyone who believes in the saving grace of Jesus's blood is home to the Lord. God resides within all believers, meaning our bodies are His temple.

> "I have the right to do anything," you say—but not everything is beneficial. "I have the right to do anything"—but I will not be mastered by anything. You say, "Food for the stomach and the stomach for food, and God will destroy them both." The body however, is not meant for sexual immorality but for the Lord, and the Lord for the body. By his power God raised the Lord from the dead, and he will raise us also. Do you not know that your bodies are members of Christ himself? Shall I then take the members of Christ and unite them with a prostitute? Never! Do you not know that he who unites himself with a prostitute is one with her body? For it is said, "The two will become one flesh." But whoever is united with the Lord is one with him in spirit.
>
> Flee from sexual immorality. All other sins a person commits are outside the body, but whoever sins sexually, sins against their own body. Do you not know that your bodies are temples of the Holy Spirit, who is in you, whom you have received from God? You are not your own; you were bought at a price. Therefore honor God with your bodies. (1 Corinthians 6:12–20 NIV)

The Bible-believing Christian certainly agrees that smoking and drinking alcohol in excess are not healthy. The difference is that because of the teachings of the Bible, the true Christian doesn't want to pollute God's body and temple.

Being a reformed smoker myself, I can recall the arrogant looks of superiority given me by those wonderfully open-minded, do-what-ever-you-wish-as-long-as-I-approve people. By making the smoker a scapegoat, we unwittingly build confidence that we are somehow superior to the tobacco user. We begin to create our own rules, and human rules are always flawed.

When we apply God's rules to anything, nothing can go wrong. The reason our society has so many problems is that our pride does not allow us to admit error. If we admit error, we admit imperfection. The more we listen to the devil, the more infallible we become in our own minds. The goal of the devil is to guide us to a point where we believe ourselves to be so mistake-free that we can now create our own morals. In other words, we no longer need God to direct us. Bingo! We have become God. The devil wins. We go to hell.

Satan can use pride in an abundance of manners.

> Where there is strife, there is pride, but wisdom is
> found in those who take advice. (Proverbs 13:10
> NIV)

Anyone too proud to admit error can actually appear quite childlike. When a child throws a tantrum, it is usually because the child is not getting his or her way or the physical object of desire at the moment. The child wants to go on that ride that is rated for kids five years older, but to the child, it doesn't matter. The child proclaims, "I have the right no matter what the ride is rated. Why can't I have that toy?" When the kid is denied something, then his or her pride is wounded and on comes the tantrum.

You, the parent, know better what is right for your children. You will do your best to teach them right from wrong. You try to protect them from the wrong outside influences. They know comparatively nothing while you have your lifetime experience and knowledge. You know better than they.

How many adults will let their six-year-old choose the restaurant they are going to dine at and the movie afterward? Do the kids make all the choices at the grocery store and then decide what's for dinner? Is the teacher taught by the pupil? No! But the child will sometimes feel things should not be the way they are. "It's just too hard, and I won't have any use for this anyway!" Is the kid right about not needing to know math, history, English, proper eating, hygiene, etc.? The pride of a child will lead to wrong decisions and a failed life.

Most of us agree with this, yet we all still exhibit pride on occasion. We still throw tantrums; we just do so in a more "adult" manner. What we tend to forget or ignore is that when we throw an adult tantrum, the results can be catastrophic. We have all had a boss, coworker, or neighbor who was not willing to accept advice due to pride. Your employer may have been struggling, and you—the person who actually does the job or hears the complaints firsthand—have, over the years, been pushing an idea to stimulate business or to reduce complaints from customers, but your boss won't listen. All you can do is roll your eyes. "Why won't the company even listen?" That darned boss is too proud to take advice from an underling.

Finally, the company implements "your" idea. Of course, your immediate supervisor takes the credit. But isn't this the same person you have been pitching to all these years? If the idea fails, you will get the credit. Either you get fired or the company closes.

But what if your idea saves the company? Your boss gets all the accolades. Maybe you get a slice of pizza and a diet cola. In the failure scenario, that boss cost himself and everybody else their jobs. In the success scenario, that darned boss unrightfully took (stole) credit while you were left with a slice of sausage and pepperoni. And you don't even like pepperoni.

The pride of that darned boss would not allow him or her to accept change, the result of which either you alone or the entire company loses. But isn't there someone else in the story guilty of pride? I could have saved the company. I saved the company. I deserve a promotion or raise. If it was indeed your idea that hammered the final nail in the company coffin, would you be willing to admit it?

Many of us have struggled with neighbors who just don't belong in "my" neighborhood. Why oh why won't they paint that porch? Maybe they just don't have the cashflow right now because they recently worked for a prideful employer. Or maybe they are afraid that old tree in your yard will fall on their porch. Yes, they have pointed out the safety concern they have about your tree. But why would you spend money to trim or remove your tree? After all, it is your tree. Besides, that porch is a real eyesore. Maybe they should remove it.

Are the porch people using your tree as an excuse (lie) not to spend money on their porch? After all, it is their porch, and they can do or not do whatever they please with it. To heck with property values in the neighborhood. They will be concerned about property values when they want to sell.

"Where there is strife, there is pride." In other words, where pride thrives, so thrives dissension and conflict. "But wisdom is found in those who take advice." In other words, open your mind and be willing to swallow your pride and accept advice from one who knows better. If you are the employer, accept the idea that can save the company and your job. If you are the employee, be grateful that your idea saved your job, even if you didn't receive a promotion. If the idea failed, at least the company respected your idea enough to implement it. By accepting the outcome, you are better able to move on.

Do the right thing for your neighbor, and you can sleep at night knowing the dispute is resolved on your end. You might even discover the most loyal neighbor and friend you never imagined.

So what is the final tale of the tape? What does all this pride stuff have to do with who we should elect to lead our nation? Well, it's really quite obvious to any true born-again believer in Christ. We were all born the same, filled with sin, and all we do is keep adding to the depth of our iniquity. The only way out is to open our minds enough to swallow our pride and accept the gift offering that Jesus Christ, the Savior of the world, provides.

God the Father is the teacher. He is the parent. He makes the rules. We are the children who don't know any better. When we decide we don't need his teachings, that we know better, our pride (like that of the child) will lead to wrong decisions and a failed afterlife, which is an eternity away from God. To be away from God means to be in hell. There is no gray area between the two. There is only with him or away from him. You cannot be kinda married, kinda pregnant, or kinda in heaven. You are married or not, pregnant or not, within heaven or not.

Once we are saved, we will want to develop a close and lasting relationship with our newfound Father. When this happens, we are letting the Holy Spirit lead us. The Spirit will guide us in discerning the truth. When a political leader goes through the same change, he or she will begin to see the truth, and the person's leadership will reflect this in a more consistent support of biblical, spiritual ideals.

A good example of this type of leader would be President Trump. In his earlier days, he was a great champion of abortion. He was a crude, coarse man addicted to the powerful sin of idolizing financial gain. He was a pillar of antibiblical values. Upon taking the office of president, Donald Trump did not exactly tone down his harsh personality, and he continues to sin in the flesh exactly like every other person on the planet. Donald Trump didn't win office by fronting a campaign platform based on antibiblical values. He won by garnering the votes of the people who will vote for a leader who generally agrees with their biblically based social values.

But is Donald Trump a believer? Even though he made a campaign promise to end public funding of Planned Parenthood, Trump signed an omnibus spending bill in March 2018 that included continued government funding of the queen mother of abortion: Planned Parenthood. An omnibus bill is a type of bill that incorporates many smaller bills into one bloated conglomeration seldom read by anyone in Congress or elsewhere. This particular omnibus was 2,232 pages, most of which was read by no member of Congress prior to voting on it. The possibility that Trump is still wet behind the ears as a Christian may have something to do with his signing this monstrosity. Many other alleged Christian conservatives, however, placed it on his desk.

While the bill increases funding for the military, and is strong on military equipment (planes, ships, and tanks), it allows criminal illegal aliens the right to run free within the United States. The bill allows child molesters, rapists, murderers, and drug dealers to continue practicing their trade and criminal political leaders to harbor these thugs and felons with no threat of punishment. The bill eliminates all funding for the southern border defense wall. So our government has opened our borders and given the blessing for any and all criminals and terrorists to come in. We will not arrest them or prevent them from committing their vile acts. This bill is certainly stupid, but stupidity and gross incompetence are not necessarily sins of the Spirit.

A Christian voter understands that a politician is a person who sins in the flesh. A Christian also understands that crucial difference between fleshly physical sin and the unforgivable sin of the Spirit. The sin of the Spirit is, of course, the rejection of God's teaching, which is ultimately the rejection of God.

When election time rolls around, there will be a number of issues to consider, many of which will concern the state (Caesar) and still not disenfranchise us from our obligations to God. There will certainly be economics, employment figures, tax rates, infrastructure, and the like, and we must consider these godly issues to a certain degree. Will a booming economy with a low unemployment rate make a nation great again at the expense of everlasting salvation? Even the unofficial credo of the military "God, country, family" puts the Creator first, and the military is generally the most patriotic portion of government employees.

If these members of the armed forces who ooze patriotism understand that God is most important, there should be no reason for one who goes to church and claims to be a faithful believer to put God anywhere but number one as well. Of course, if this churchgoing believer is only that—a "churchgoing believer"—there is little reason to be surprised that this individual would place God somewhere other than number one.

Are you thinking *Did I miss something? Why would a "churchgoing believer" rank God down on the list?* Because going to church does not save anybody. Those who are saved will want to go to church to worship their number one and to learn and grow in their faith. For the saved, going to church is not an obligation to make sure they get to heaven. God isn't holding a calculator while souls are coming into glory. When a person is forming a relationship with the Lord, it's the relationship that counts, not the number of times he or she showed up on Sunday.

There are many who memorize scripture and have a thorough knowledge of the Bible in their heads. But knowledge and understanding are two different things. Mindful knowledge without heartfelt understanding means nothing. Scripture is just words to someone without the Holy Spirit. True belief comes when the Spirit resides in the heart. The gospel of Luke sums up "churchgoing believers" quite efficiently.

> Jesus said "Strive to enter through the narrow door; for many, I tell you, will seek to enter and will not be able. Once the head of house gets up and shuts the door, and you begin to stand outside and knock on the door, saying, 'Lord, open up to us!' then He will answer and say to you, 'I do not know where you are from.'" (Luke 13:23–24 NASB)

> Then you will begin to say, "We ate and drank in your presence, and you taught in our streets"; and he will say "I tell you, I do not know where you are from; depart from me, all you evildoers." (Luke 13:26–27 NASB)

Just going through the motions is not a relationship with God. Head knowledge means nothing without acceptance in the heart, which means swallowing our pride and allowing God to make us into new creations. Holding onto past beliefs is holding onto the beliefs of man. Remember, God the Father knows better, but we must seek him with our hearts.

> In his pride the wicked man does not seek him; in all his thoughts there is no room for God. (Psalm 10:4 NIV)

We are all physically born into the world. So how can we become new creations? We need to allow God to scrap who we are. We must let him take all our old beliefs and ask him to make us new. This means letting him replace a lifetime of beliefs. That takes a bit of humility, not pride!

> Now there was a Pharisee, a man named Nicodemus who was a member of the Jewish ruling council. He came to Jesus at night and said, "Rabbi, we know you are a teacher that has come from God. For no one could perform the signs you are doing if God were not with him." Jesus replied, "Very truly I tell you, no one can see the kingdom of God unless they are born again." How can someone be born when they are old?" Nicodemus asked. "Surely they cannot enter a second time into their mother's womb to be born." Jesus answered, "Very truly I tell you, no one can enter the kingdom of God unless they are born of water and the Spirit. Flesh gives birth to flesh, but the Spirit gives birth to spirit. You should not be surprised at my saying, 'You must be born again.' (John 3:1–7 NIV)

Those who have been born again, of course, still live in this world. The body still breathes, and the heart continues to pump blood through the circulatory system. It is the soul, the real person, the person on the inside, that is reborn. This is the person who will continue on after the mortal body dies.

The eternal person is reborn as a brand-new creation, an everlasting child of the one true God, the God of Abraham, Isaac, and Jacob, the single God who came to earth in the form of a man to save us all by paying our sin debt for us so we could spend eternity with him. When our soul is recreated as God's child, we have been born a second time.

When we are born again, we see the world in a new light. We see the world through the eyes of the Savior. We see the evil he sees, but we are still imperfect humans who can be tempted by the devil. We must always remember that we are all sinners alike. We are no better than the worst sinner. We are just forgiven sinners whom God wants to use to reach others who have not yet asked forgiveness.

None of us are worthy to stand in the presence of God, but he extends an invitation to each and every one of us. When we have been born a second time, we are able to see the world in a way we were not able to see before we were born again. Previous to our rebirth, we saw the world in the same way those who are not saved still see. When we are saved, it becomes our responsibility to allow the Holy Spirit to use us to guide nonbelievers into the light of knowledge of the Savior, so they may see the way we now see.

When we try to get those of the world to come to our world-view, they will perceive us as narrow-minded and self-serving bigots. It is the Christian, however, who has opened his or her mind to consider an alternate view. It is the Christian who risks persecution to guide others into eternal glory with the Lord. It is the Christian who opens his or her heart to all the world.

It is the closed-minded and the selfish who deny us our faith. Hatred is for the unreborn. Love is for the reborn. Is it right to elect leaders who prosper in the world's view? We must not be fooled by the devil. He will try to make obvious the sin of a candidate he despises. We should recognize this as the same sin we have. We all make mistakes. As true Christians, we must swallow our pride and view our choices in the light of God's truth. The right choice should not support antibiblical worldviews.

> For the word of the cross is foolishness to those who are perishing, but to us who are being saved it is the power of God. (1 Corinthians 1:18 NASB)

> But a natural man does not accept the things of the Spirit of God, for they are foolishness to him;

and he cannot understand them, because they are
spiritually appraised. (1 Corinthians 2:14 NASB)

Think about it. Are you a self-professing Christian who is allowing the pride of the devil to dictate your decisions? Do you support
leadership you know to be upholding worldviews that oppose the
spiritual view of God? Do you support a political party or candidate who bathes the White House in a rainbow of light to celebrate
gay marriage? Do you still favor a candidate who approves of killing
babies at full development, as long as a portion of the child is still
within his or her mother's womb? Are you willing to cast a ballot in
favor of a candidate who believes the Bible has no place in our public
society? Are you prepared to cast a vote for a political candidate or
party that openly rejects the spiritual view?

Although no human being with a little D or a little R in front
of his or her name can save America or the world, God can use that
person for good, or Satan can use that person for bad. When we support the bad, can it be an indication that we are not of the good? Not
if we believe the devil. He says we're just being open-minded.

> Jesus said to them, "If God were your father, you
> would love Me, for I proceeded forth and have
> come from God, for I have not even come on
> My own initiative, but He sent Me. Why do you
> not understand what I am saying? It is because
> you cannot hear My word. You are of your father
> the devil, and you want to do the desires of your
> father. He was a murderer from the beginning,
> and does not stand in the truth because there is
> no truth in him. Whenever he speaks a lie, he
> speaks from his own nature, for he is a liar and
> the father of lies. But because I speak the truth,
> you do not believe me. (John 8:42–45 NASB)

Is it so simple to vindicate evil for those who are truly in the
light of righteousness?

Those of us who reside in the everlasting light of God will almost always feel the guilt of our conscience when we sin, or allow our pride to let us look the other way at sin's occurrence. We of the light realize the feeling of guilt is actually the Holy Spirit residing within us, notifying us of the error of our ways.

When the Spirit gives us this feeling of guilt, it is the spiritual version of our sensory nerves giving the sensation of pain when we put our hand in the fire. When we put our hand in the flame, that portion of our physical body gets burned. It hurts! Our body is warning us. But this fire damage will heal in time. Our guilt is warning us that we are in danger of a more permanent type of burning.

If we are not getting the spiritual alert when we sin, it may be because the Spirit isn't living in us to alert us. Once we allow our pride to turn our heads from sin, with no regret, such as when we permit godless governing by our leaders, we have condoned sin. A true Christian will find condolence of sin more than a little distasteful and fight it at all costs. Does that small D in front of a candidate's name mean more than the truth?

> He who is of God hears the words of God; for
> this reason you do not hear them, because you
> are not of God. (John 8:47 NASB)

Do you hear the words of God, yet still choose to follow your pride? If you do, you might be in danger of an everlasting scorching. But accepting Jesus can cool things down more than anyone can imagine.

Everyone is capable of judgment. While it is not part of any human responsibility to judge another of sin, it is the responsibility of all who are saved to spread the word to those who are not saved. Because God wants to reach all of us, he gives those in his light the ability to discern who needs to hear of him and who just needs to grow in maturity of their faith.

When we are born again, we may be on our way to heaven, but we are still newborn infants. This new life is exciting and joyous, but we are still babies, and we need to grow by praying by talking to God, by associating with other more mature Christians, and by persistent Bible study.

As we grow into spiritual adulthood, we find our blessings more abundant. We understand when our heavenly Father is teaching us. When he is disciplining us, we understand it is for our own good and for his glory. And we learn to recognize those who have not yet abandoned their old lives in favor of the new birth that brings everlasting joy.

When the apostle Paul wrote to those in the church in Corinth, he expressed his concern that they were not growing in their faith. Like immature Christians today, many in ancient Corinth were easily fooled into believing the wrong things.

> Brothers and sisters, I could not address you as people who live by the Spirit but as people who are still worldly—mere infants in Christ. I gave you milk, not solid food, for you were not yet ready for it. Indeed, you are still not ready. You are still worldly. For since there is jealousy and quarreling among you, are you not worldly? Are you not acting like mere humans? For when one says, "I follow Paul," and another, "I follow Apollos," are you not mere human beings? (1 Corinthians 3:1–4 NIV)

In other words, some in the church at Corinth were dedicating themselves to the teachings of Paul, while others were following Apollos. They were more interested in the teaching methods of a particular person and, therefore, completely missed the truth. They were supposed to be focusing on the teachings of Jesus.

Paul, like today's teachers, was simply allowing the Holy Spirit to use him to teach the truth. When we start worshiping the pastor, priest, or minister, we are making the human being the real God. We become deceived and lose touch with the real God.

Although some teachers are better than others, they are still just following orders of the Holy Spirit. The difference between a good teacher and a bad one is easy to determine. The bad doesn't follow orders. The bad teacher allows human ideas to influence his or her teaching. But if you don't study the word on your own, how can you identify faulty instruction? When we are reborn, we need to open up to the Spirit and allow ourselves to mature.

You see, God gave us an advocate, a messenger if you will, to relay the truth between us and God. That messenger is the Holy Spirit, who takes up residence in us when we accept Christ. When we put our faith in the wrong place, we will undoubtedly begin to fall from grace. This is just what the devil wants. When we put all our eggs in one basket, and it is the wrong basket, trouble will ensue. That wrong basket may be someone with a little D or R in front of his or her name. If we aren't listening to the advocate God has given us, we will believe things that sound as if they must be right with the Lord. Many, many times, however, these things are contrary to God's instruction.

Most with the D and many with the R are not listening to the advocate and, therefore, are not leading righteously. Almost all on the far-left have completely rejected the advocate. They are actually admonishing godless national doctrine with the full support of a nation of infantile Christians. These supposed Christians are slitting their own throats. Each of us must be brutally honest with ourselves. Are we allowing pride in our own human reasoning to draw a knife near our eternal throats?

Although Epaphras is credited with bringing the gospel to the city of Colossae, Paul later wrote to the established church there. While Paul's letter primarily addressed some incidents of false teaching, his letter also provides a good explanation of the duty of the Holy Spirit.

> We continually ask God to fill you with the knowledge of his will through all the wisdom and understanding that the Spirit gives, so that you may live a life worthy of the Lord and please him in every way: bearing fruit in every good work, growing in the knowledge of God, being

strengthened with all power according to his glorious might so that you may have great endurance and patience, and giving joyful thanks to the Father, who has qualified you to share in the inheritance of his holy people in the kingdom of light. For he has rescued us from the dominion of darkness and brought us into the kingdom of the Son he loves, in whom we have redemption, the forgiveness of sins. (Colossians 1:9–14 NIV)

"We continually ask God to fill you with the knowledge of his will through all the wisdom and understanding that the Spirit gives." If you don't know the Spirit, how can you receive the knowledge? When your child receives that first math book, the knowledge won't just appear in the kid's mind. The book must be opened and studied. Then the blessings will come. Perhaps it may lead to a productive life as a mathematician or an accountant. If that textbook remains closed, the mind cannot absorb it.

The brain is, in effect, acting as the advocate. The difference between this advocate and the Holy Spirit is the information the textbook provides can only help us during our short span in our earthly bodies. Some human textbooks can even deter us from believing the truth by teaching falsehoods involving creation and evolution, as well as altering accurate biblical history and even the Christian heritage of our own nation.

By corrupting our children's schoolbooks, the devil can get a head start on convincing our children to condemn themselves to hell. One would expect a parent to want to understand the true teachings in the Bible and to want to teach them to their children. The Bible is the one textbook that means more than all the others combined.

Jesus himself told of the importance of the advocate in the gospel of John.

Unless I go away, the Advocate will not come to you; but if I go, I will send him to you. When he comes, he will prove the world to be wrong about sin and righteous and judgment: about sin, because people do not believe in me; about righteousness, because I am going to the Father, where you can see me no longer; and about judgment, because the prince of this world (Satan) now stands condemned. (John 16:7–11 NIV)

As we have just seen, the advocate (the Holy Spirit) will accomplish three tasks:

1. Make us aware of our sin of disbelief.
2. Make us understand that through repentance and belief in Jesus's death and resurrection, we can be in a right standing with God.
3. Make us understand that Satan has been condemned. In other words, the way of the world has been judged.

A simplified version of the three tasks:

1. If we don't believe and repent from our hearts, we will be condemned.
2. Only belief in Jesus and true repentance can save us.
3. If we don't believe and repent, we will join Satan.

If we ignore the Spirit, we won't grow stronger in faith. If we don't grow stronger in faith, we will absolutely not be clearsighted enough to resist the lies and temptations of the devil.

When we silence the righteous messenger from Jesus, Satan will lead us astray. At this point, the devil can use us as his heart desires. One thing he will do is use us to draw others away from the Savior. If our leaders offer us the candy of entitlements and we go for the sweetness, he has us.

Although not every entitlement is a bad thing, enough of them can entice us to a political ideal stronger in preponderance to us than our faith in the Savior. When this happens, *boom*: Satan has us in his filthy claws.

Anytime a government official, political party, or governmental doctrine subscribes to antibiblical standards or establishments, they are unabashedly declining support to God. When "we the people" agree with these individuals, groups, and policies, we are also giving God the raspberry.

When a group of people who identify as Christian reject the Lord due to an unwillingness to accept correction, they are demonstrating their lack of backbone. Their support of Christ is spineless and wormlike. This is what happens when we let our pride rule our decision-making. This kind of pride actually seals off our ability to open our minds, which is needed if we wish to say "no" to our earthly delights in sin and say "yes" to letting God turn us into new creations. God knows everything about us. We cannot keep anything secret from him. If we decide to succumb to our earthly desires and continue to support any agenda that is detrimental to our following God's word, God will know about it.

> But a certain man named Ananias, with Sapphira his wife, sold a possession. And he kept back part of the proceeds, his wife also being aware of it, and brought a certain part and laid it at the apostles' feet. But Peter said "Ananias, why has Satan filled your heart to lie to the Holy Spirit and keep back part of the price of the land for yourself? While it remained, was it not your own? And after it was sold, was it not in your own control? Why have you conceived this thing in your heart? You have not lied to men but God." Then Ananias, hearing these words, fell down and breathed his last. (Acts 5:1–5 NKJV)

Ananias made his pledge to give to the Lord. He chose to hold back what he promised God. If he believed he could sneak one past God, he did not have God in his heart. If he had true faith, he would have understood that he could not keep any secrets. Besides, all that we have is God's. When we keep for ourselves what we promised him, we are actually stealing from him.

But the story continues. What of Ananias's wife, Sapphira?

> Now it was about three hours later when his wife came in, not knowing what had happened. And Peter answered her, "Tell me whether you sold the land for so much?" She said, "Yes, for so much." Then Peter said to her, "How is it that you have agreed together to test the Spirit of the Lord? Look, the feet of those who have buried your husband *are* at the door, and they will carry you out." Then immediately she fell down at his feet and breathed her last. And the young men came in and found her dead, and carrying *her* out, buried *her* by her husband. (Acts 5:7–10 NKJV)

None of us can hide anything. We can only place our sin at his feet and request disposal. Although we don't see many people being instantly struck down today, our sin is nonetheless convicting us. We mustn't allow pride to convince us that we can keep secrets from God, even in the ballot box. Nobody needs to know how we vote. It is our own choice to vote as we pray, or to pray one way and vote another way. Before we punch that hole or pull that lever for that candidate who holds to a politically correct but biblically incorrect platform, we need to remember that God knows how we vote.

Voting for a candidate who rides a platform of paganism makes you or me every bit as guilty as the candidate. Ignorance is not an excuse. If we claim to be Christian yet support anti-Christian agendas, then we are putting that agenda ahead of Christ. Why is that agenda so difficult to deny? Simple. All those discussions that turned into heated arguments at election time. How could you possibly admit error now? And your answer is staring you in the face. P-R-I-D-E! Don't allow the devil to drag you down to his level. Let the Holy Spirit lead you to strengthen your faith in God and eliminate that pride so you can better see the truth.

Is it right for a person who claims to be Christian to shame Donald Trump for altering his belief system? The Christian who derides Trump as being inconsistent and a liar is attacking him for finally, later in his life, accepting the Savior, something the supposed Christian had already personally done. When the Christian critic of the president rejected sin and became a new creation in the Lord, was that person accused of inconsistency and hatred? If that individual truly accepted the Lord, that person would likely see the world in a new light. Then why would that Christian attack another believer? The answer could be that the Christian critic is not saved at all.

Trump may still be wet behind the ears as a Christian, but his faith is strong enough to allow him to place himself in the crosshairs of a great many God-haters in order to stand strong and thankful to his, our, and their Creator.

If the Christian who chastises Trump had read the Bible, the story of Saul would be the enlightenment needed to end the unchristian assault on a fellow believer. Those who profess to be Christian, yet are ignorant of Saul, are either kidding themselves about their Christianity or are newborn infants in their faith and in desperate need of growth and maturity.

Saul, better known as Paul to the biblically informed, was and is the grand symbolic model of an Antichrist turned pro-Christ. He stood by and watched the belongings of the ones who stoned Stephen to death for preaching the truth of the Savior.

Saul was the purest specimen of a Jesus-hating student of the prophets and the books of Moses. He read, thoroughly understood, and believed. Exactly like many Christians who read and believe today, Saul was deceived by the devil and failed to recognize the Savior spoken of by the prophets. Jesus filled the criteria to claim messiahship to the last detail. No hint of exactness was wanting in the fulfillment of the prophecy of the coming Messiah that Jesus did not fill. Jesus is truly the Christ.

Saul certainly believed in God and was determined to stand for the law of God in the face of what he believed to be any false Messiah. That old liar of liars, Satan himself, managed to blind Saul to the evidence of the truth of the new covenant that Messiah Jesus brought.

Just as many people today refuse to see and correct the error in their judgment, and continue down the path of pride and ignorance to revel in antibiblical views of issues on abortion, marriage, creationism, and religious freedom, Saul hardened his heart against Jesus. God used Saul as the ultimate illustration to all of us of his capability to soften the hardest of hearts. But, and this is a big but, we have to allow the softening agent of the Holy Spirit to perform the tenderizing. We must accept it and welcome him in.

Saul was not even contemplating softening his heart when he left Jerusalem for Damascus. His mission was to seize followers of Jesus and return them to the high priests in the temple at Jerusalem for judgment. God needed to deal with these rabble rousers severely.

> As he neared Damascus on his journey, suddenly a light from heaven flashed around him. He fell to the ground and heard a voice say to him, "Saul, Saul, why do you persecute me?" "Who are you, Lord?" Saul asked. "I am Jesus, whom you are persecuting," he replied. "Now get up and go into the city, and you will be told what you must do." (Acts 9:3–6 NIV)

Those who were traveling with Saul heard the noise but did not understand that it was a language, nor did they see anything. As for Saul, he came out of the incident physically blind, but God had granted him his spiritual sight. He now saw the light of truth and stepped into it fully.

Saul's traveling companions led him on to Damascus. He stayed in a home on straight street owned by one called Judas. While Saul was at the house, God gave him a dream, and a believer named Ananias a vision. Saul's dream notified him of Ananias coming to him to restore his sight. Ananias's vision instructed him to go to Saul for that purpose. Ananias was familiar with Saul's track record. He knew Saul's obsession was to capture and eliminate believers of Jesus, and he reminded God of this. Ananias was, in all likelihood, fearful of visiting Saul. After all, few possessed Saul's fervor to wipe out Jesus followers.

> But the Lord said to Ananias, "Go! This man is my chosen instrument to proclaim my name to the Gentiles and their kings and to the people of Israel. I will show him how much he must suffer for my name." (Acts 9:15–16 NIV)

Ananias dutifully obeyed and went to Saul. Following instructions, Ananias placed his hands on Saul. His sight was restored, and the Holy Spirit filled him to capacity. He immediately went out to the synagogues to tell them of the truth of Jesus.

I'll give the reader one guess what the reaction of the nonbelievers was. Just like the nonbelievers of today, they hatched a plan to kill Saul. How dare Saul open his mind to the possibility of God being more knowledgeable than they? No, the feasibility of Saul continuing to live after changing his mind was out of the question.

These Christians teaching all this love and repentance had to go. The Pharisees saw no virtue in them. That was then, and this is now. Replace the Pharisees, Sadducees, Essenes, Zealots, and Romans with prochoice, nontraditional marriage and the gay agenda, Hollywood, the mainstream media, and anyone else who does not believe.

The examples of Christian persecution today are endless. Overseas, Christians are being beheaded, burned alive, roasted on spits, crucified, and drowned in cages dunked into the sea. Babies are being crucified. Anti-Semitism is escalating worldwide. Anyone care to forget the Holocaust so soon? Leaders of Islamic nations such as Iran chant "Death to America! Death to Israel!" What is the link that chains America and Israel together? We both believe in the one true God, the God of Abraham, Isaac, and Jacob. Simplistically, the only difference between true Christians and true Jews is that the Jew awaits the coming of the Messiah. The Christian awaits the second coming of the Messiah—the same Messiah, Jesus Christ. It was originally the task of the Jew to give the word to the Gentile. Now it is the duty of the Christian to give the word to the Jew.

Satan hates God. It is the nonbeliever who has been duped by the devil to hate the Christian and the Jew. If the nonbeliever believed, this truth would instantly become evident.

Many believe America could never be the home to atrocities similar to those occurring elsewhere in the world. But look at what occurs at Christian prolife prayer rallies. Prochoice left-wingers hurl insults and carry signs brandishing the foulest language directed at the Christians and their "hateful" God. On many occasions, the choicers throw rocks at the peaceful group meditating in prayer for the lives of the babies at stake and the healing of the pain of the mothers who opt to have the procedure.

Pay attention to the next prochoice or prohomosexuality gathering or march. You will see anger and hate in those present. Their eyes will be filled with contempt for any who disagree. Then view the video of a prolife or protraditional marriage gathering (if the media even provides any coverage). You will notice smiles and joy. You will not hear any cussing, other than that which emits from the mouths of the other side in their attempt to bleed a remark of human weakness from the believer.

The observance of these two different behaviors should at least convince the open-minded outsider that the real hate-mongers are not visibly the Christians.

Saul was an early example of a persecutor of Christians, and his story of conversion is the ultimate demonstration of the power of God to heal satanic behavior. Saul had dedicated his life to extinguishing believers of Jesus. Because he was able to swallow his pride, he now lives with the Lord.

> Then *Saul, who was also called Paul,* filled with the Holy Spirit, looked straight at Elymas and said, "You are a child of the devil and an enemy of everything that is right! You are full of all kinds of deceit and trickery. Will you never stop perverting the right ways of the Lord? (Acts 13:9 NIV)

Saul, the butcher of Jesus followers, became *Paul,* the missionary of Christ. Saul, the hater, allowed the Holy Spirit in and was transformed into Paul, whom God would inspire to write thirteen books of the New Testament. Yes, the Paul of the Bible was the Saul of the Bible!

It only takes an authentic open mind to give God a chance. A narrow thinker is a person whose thoughts are contaminated by the lies of the devil. If Satan has his way, the perverted truth of his dubious character will be deeply infused in our own land of the free. The indications are clear that we are rejecting the truth of God in favor of the lies of the devil. As examples, I submit the following: Not long ago, the Christian-owned restaurant chain Chick-Fil-A announced it was going to open a location in a neighborhood of Chicago. Joe Moreno, the alderman of the ward where the restaurant was to open, viciously attacked the ownership of the restaurant chain and any and all Christians. He did not want to allow this bunch of narrow-minded haters to open a location in his ward.

Chicago Mayor Rahm Emmanuel echoed Moreno's sentiments, stating "Chick-fil-A values are not Chicago values.⁷" The same city is cited twice as an example of Satan's anger. Chicago is a city plagued by violence and crime in the early twenty-first century. I myself was held up at gunpoint in a Chicago city park.

When President Trump offered assistance from United States Marshals, Mayor Rahm Emmanuel rejected the help. People are dying in droves, yet Mayor Emmanuel placed his politics first and rejected the aid. Instead, he called to make Chicago a sanctuary city for illegal felons. As the population of Chicago dwindles due to astoundingly high crime rates, overzealous taxation, and outrageous corruption, the mayor sought to replace the fleeing masses by providing sanctuary to drug dealers, murderers, rapists, and child molesters.

This is the behavior of a man so filled with pride that he would sooner risk destruction of a once-thriving metropolis than admit error and plead for the return of God. He would rather invite criminals than accept the help of a man who once thought along the same lines but who eventually stepped into the light.

While President Trump may not deserve similar accolades as Paul, their stories are similar. Both strongly rejected God. Both spit out their pride. Both received vile attacks and the threat of death from those who once rode the same boat. Trump, like Paul, like all believers, jumped ship before it sailed over the falls into eternal damnation. The story of Paul is the story of all who accept the grace offering of the Savior.

In August 1984, President Ronald Reagan said in Dallas, Texas, "Without God, there's no virtue, because there's no prompting of the conscience. Without God, we're mired in the material, that flat world that tells us only what the senses perceive. Without God, there is a coarsening of the society. And without God, democracy will not and cannot long endure. If we ever forget that we're One Nation under God, then we will be a nation gone under."

When political parties take the place of God, hatred levels soar. Too many people, including those calling themselves "Christians," are sickened by those offenders from that other political party. Think about it using Christian ideals, if you really possess them, and you will know you are guilty. As President Reagan stated, the coarsening of our society is due to a rejection of God en masse.

If you want to vote the way you pray, you need to reject your worship of human political parties and refocus on worshiping your Savior. The next time you feel the need to turn on CNN, open the New York Times, or think you're going to learn anything from a narrow-minded hateful "news" outlet, swallow your pride and open your Bible instead. Don't believe me or anyone else. Get your news from God's word. If you accept what he has to say, you will learn how to vote. But first, you need to pick up your pride by the seat of its pants and just say "no" to the opinion peddlers on your television or your Internet!

The bottom line is that because of our human pride, we find it arduous to change. When we are set in our ways, we convince ourselves that these are the right methods to live by since we have always believed them to be the successful route. Deep down, we all feel we are a little smarter than the next guy, but those of us who live by the Holy Spirit will quickly get a nudge from our conscience, and we will correct course. When we put credence into the idea that we are somehow better than another, we place ourselves in the place of God. If I can judge like God, then I don't need God.

Satan is the spark to ignite our pride and uses it to suck us down many sinful trails. The desire to have a better car than the neighbor leads to greed. The need for a trophy wife or husband leads to lust. The want of a prestigious title at work leads to mistrust and power grabs. When we zero-in on these things, Satan is steering us away from God. These things dictate all our decisions.

Satan can even use our anger. Anger is a form of mind-altering drug. A perfectly calm individual can become a wild maniac devoid of any composure at the sudden onset of anger. Most folks attempt to justify anger, and, in most cases, anger is a realization of something deemed to be threatening or insulting. In reality, the incident that caused the eruption of anger is seldom threatening. It is usually a comment or action that offends our pride. When pride is aroused from its slumber, the devil grabs hold of it and attaches it to something we hold dear, such as a parking spot or that place in the checkout at the grocery store. It is amazing what incidental little nothings blow up into raging tantrums.

Operating a vehicle five or six days per week, for example, is a tough way to make a living. But in toast to Mike Rowe at Trinity Broadcast Network, "Somebody's got to do it." Being a professional driver in a large city can be quite stressful, even maddening. I eventually reached a point of numbness to the selfish, rude, and dangerous actions of others sharing the road. The things people do when behind the wheel border on the macabre. The bizarre thought patterns of some drivers can be enough to drive a good Christian to church. If that's the case, let's hear it for all the lousy drivers out there.

Like most professional drivers who don't crack, I became jaded. I don't recall the exact conjuncture when it happened, but at some point, I just did not care anymore. Another driver could purposely try to run me off the road, give me the finger, and shout some penetrating closed-window vocal obscenities all because the car in front of me slowed down to turn, which, in turn, caused me to reduce speed. I had seen crashes from stupid mistakes and from road rage.

I once saw a bus sideswiped and forced into a crowd of pedestrians, resulting in at least one death.

My hundreds of thousands of hours behind the wheel left me in a state of complacent unconcern. But I am only flesh, and Satan is patient. He sat quiet until the opportunity arrived. He knew precisely when my guard would be down, and he aroused my pride and attached it to my anger.

As I drove to work one morning, the driver of another car decided he was just a little more important than the rest of us on that morning rush hour. He pulled into a closed lane and slingshot himself ahead of about twenty cars. I was the one he cut in front of. Normally, this would have been a mild annoyance to be forgotten in a few minutes, but not this time. This selfish behavior irked me to no end. I wallowed in it the entire day. I imagined myself dragging him out of his car and telling him what I and everybody else on the road thought of him. It didn't end at that.

My mind's eye broadcast my fist making contact with his face while the police read him his rights. He probably did deserve a traffic citation, but my add-ons were maybe a bit much. For some reason, the incident would not leave me alone. It nagged me hour after hour. My anger simmered while the offensive driver probably never cared what he did and not once thought about his actions. He didn't know the color of my vehicle, even though I could recall every last detail of his car and his now-disfigured face as I wiped his blood off my knuckles.

That night, as I retired for the evening, the event of the morning still dominated my thoughts. Sleep would not come easy. The tossing and turning was relentless. Finally, I heard something that I'm certain was being broadcast at full volume all day. The Holy Spirit pierced my pride. The realization that I needed to forgive this person came to the forefront. It is my belief that the words Jesus used in teaching us how to pray can be used in any circumstance. As I lay in bed, unable to sleep, I began reciting the Lord's prayer, only I customized it to the driver of that other car. Then I customized it for another acquaintance I felt needed prayer. Again, I reiterated the prayer for another. Then another, and another, and another. I prayed the Lord's prayer for family and friends whose salvation with God I doubted, and for those I felt confident were in the way and manner of Jesus. People came to mind one after the next, and there didn't seem to be a gap between the completion of one prayer and the beginning of the next.

I could not stop. I felt the Spirit urging me to continue, and he always brought another name to mind. The need to pray for some and forgive others felt unstoppable. It just kept coming, and there seemed no way to slow it. The urge to help, forgive, and be forgiven was Spirit-breathed. It welled up in me to a point where it could not be contained. The names and prayers seemed endless, yet I felt no despair. I yearned for another. I didn't want it to end. In an instant, my mind was frozen. My head jerked back in the pillow with the startling, instantaneous appearance of a face. The prayers halted as I gazed at the face of a man with many years behind him. His hair was as white as snow and receded a bit, as one might expect of any senior. It was dreamlike and, at the same time, as real as anything I could reach out and touch.

The brightness around the face was blinding, yet it did not bother my sight. It seemed to prevent me from seeing and focusing on anything other than the face. It was not a photograph-like image, as motion could somehow be detected. The face bared a slight smile, not a toothy laughing sort of smile, but more of an "I'm pleased" kind of smile. My subconscious memory indicates the ever-so-min-ute nod of satisfaction accompanying the smile.

As suddenly as he appeared, he vanished. I have no words to explain it. He disappeared quicker than lightspeed. I can't describe just how faster than the speed of light it happened. It is something I could only experience. He was gone, and I was wide awake. My eyes did not need to adjust to the coming of the light or the going of the light. The vision lasted probably ten to fifteen seconds, but my reaction lasted a little longer. I simply remained motionless. I realized my mouth was agape, and I had no idea what had just occurred. I looked through the darkness about the room and assured myself that I was awake.

Then I began to understand some of what the vision was all about. I thought about the morning incident on the road. My anger had dissipated. Peace was with me, but I had to test it. At first, I felt a certain hesitance to test the work of God, but the notion came (I'm sure from the Spirit) that it would be okay. I attempted to relive the incident in my mind and to justify my anger at this person's indiscriminate indifference to me and every other motorist on the road. His rudeness was infuriatingly self-evident. I attempted to recreate the rage I felt all day.

But it wasn't happening. I had forgiven this man, and the anger was gone. The hatred I would not release persisted in harassing me all day and into the night. It threatened to hover over me forever. It was simple forgiveness that destroyed all that animosity. It was eliminated so completely that years later, I can recall that morning in all its detail, and no emotion other than peace is activated within me. So while the incident is clear in my memory, the anger has been washed away as if it had never existed.

I wonder if this could be what God is speaking of when he says that our sin will still linger, but he will forgive it as if it never happened.

> Their sins and lawless acts I will remember no more. (Hebrews 10:17 NIV)

Our transgressions will not go away, for we have committed them, and we will pay the price here in this life. An adulterous relationship or a theft will lead to penalties, such as divorce or jail time. The sin will continue to haunt us while we live, yet God will forget it if our repentance is genuine and our belief in Jesus's work is real.

We must never forget that our good works mean nothing because we are also the owners of bad works (sin). Jesus performed the only work that can wash away our evil a couple thousand years ago. So how is it that I am able to recall an event that roused so much unpardonable hatred and not feel a gumdrop of animosity toward the offender today? Thanks to the power of the Almighty Creator, I was blessed with a lesson in forgiveness that could only have culminated from a rejection of my personal pride, which allowed me to pray for the forgiveness of another sinner.

In other words, I kicked my pride out the door. It is true that the other motorist was wrong in his actions, but it was pride that led to my great anger. I felt he should not have done what he did, and, instead of being in front of me, he should have trailed by twenty car lengths. Or at least he should have been behind me.

To allow my pride to transform such an insignificant event into a life-altering nightmare was absolutely devil-inspired. Satan attached pride to unrighteous anger and managed to divert me from our Savior for an entire day. Who can tell how many opportunities to share the word of God were missed because the devil had a true believer distracted? And that is exactly why Satan will still attack true believers. If we don't tell of Jesus as we are commanded, Satan can continue to round up lost souls without opposition.

The devil uses pride to control us. In our own minds, pride seems a necessary function of self-defense. But in reality, the proud man is one who exhibits the inability to admit error. When we make a mistake at work, for example, many times we are not prepared to admit guilt. Our pride requires us to deflect blame in order to make ourselves appear more competent. It is to the detriment of the proud to swagger over others, as this infuses the braggart with an elevating self-righteousness. Many people, for example, exaggerate their income or responsibility of their employment position to place themselves above another. The devil can easily use this raised evaluation of self to impart self-confidence levels, which can lead to a sense of power, relegating the need of a Savior to secondary status.

Even if you do have a greater salary than someone else, this will lead to greed because the need to stay ahead financially means more work. The next thing you know, your job has become an obsession, which is another way of calling it a false idol.

In the midst of a ninety-minute commute home from the office, it may seem crucial to remain one car length ahead. Letting the other car in ahead of us can delay us by…well, it really won't delay us at all. After all, there are ten thousand vehicles ahead of us, and another ten thousand to our rear. It's just that it's our spot in line. At least, that is what our pride tells us. If that other car forces in, that's the opportunity for the devil to attach pride to anger.

How about the big game? To the Green Bay Packer fan who feels the need to insult the mother of the Chicago Bear fan, or to raise his fist in reaction to the outcome of a football game: it's only a game! No matter who wins on the field, on the court, or in the rink, the fan in the stands is not going to be invited to the postgame celebration and is not going to be the recipient of a championship ring.

Satan wants you to become infatuated with a sports team as a way of getting you to worship that team in place of God. Any substitution for God is a victory for Satan. If your team loses, he will use your pride to initiate hatred for the winner and supporters of said victor. Likewise, when your team wins, your pride is aroused to gloat over the fallen. Gloating is the devil's way of attacking two at the same time. Your gloating can serve to arouse anger, and then you and your rival are induced with rage, which blinds you to common sense.

So the next time you venture into a polling place, remember that if you claim Christianity as your faith, you could be purposely voting against the will of God if you cast a ballot for a candidate who represents the vile nature of Satan, and not the teachings of your Christian Lord. When a political leader supports what God does not support, that leader is supporting what the devil supports. When a person supports that unrighteous politician, that person is supporting the devil.

One who knows God's word understands that God can't be left out of the decision process. This person can see a leader who does not know or rejects God's word because one who knows God's word can determine if another knows God's word. One who knows God's word may still fail to obey it but will understand their error and repent. If the request of forgiveness is genuine, God will grant it. The disobedience will, however, result in negative consequences on earth. One who does not know God's word, however, cannot obey God's word. Those who refuse to swallow their pride and learn for themselves what the word of God has to say may as well jump on the devil's party wagon because the express jet to heaven has left. But God is always prepared to detour it back, just for you.

If your pride tells you not to read the word of God, you will be guilty of siding against Jesus. If you really do have the Holy Spirit resting inside you, your conscience will lead you to the desire to read the Bible, for that conscience is the voice of the Spirit of God. The Holy Spirit is your conscience.

A true Christian who is looking forward to eternity with the Savior does not put his or her faith aside after an hour on Sunday. Attending a church service once a week is not a successful method of defeating the influence of the devil if the remaining 167 hours of the week are dedicated to Satan's temptations. One hour of worship, which is probably not even an hour of true worship from the heart, will leave you completely defenseless to the evil charms of the great deceiver.

In the presidential election of 2016, the evangelical community made a choice. To those who don't know God's word, the result of that election was a disaster because those who have left God out of the equation throughout history have made foolish decisions.

To cast an election to the wiles of Satan is to choose to ally oneself as a true follower of him. Following Satan does not mean one does not believe in God, as there are many Satan worshipers who claim the devil is the deity who will conquer in the end. This is, however, a lie perpetrated by the devil, who knows all too well that in the end, it is the great Creator who will win out. Satan even knows there is only one deity. He is completely aware that when he looks in the mirror, he is not looking at that deity.

The devil is more aware of his outcome than any human can imagine. Even the human who reads and studies the Bible has not been around as long as Satan. So it is not hard to realize how someone who does not read the Bible can be rendered so completely and utterly helpless to the taunts of the devil.

Why does Satan continue to rebel when he knows his fate? Because he is not human, he will not be forgiven. He is an angel who started an uprising in heaven. Hell was created specifically for Satan and the third of the angels who followed him in rebellion.

We, on the other hand, were created in the image of the Lord as his children, and the devil, in his hatred for God, tempted us to sin against God. Because Adam and Eve succumbed to Satan's temptations, we are as fallen as the angels who followed Satan. Unlike Satan and his fallen angels, however, we are offered the gift of grace, which means we can be forgiven, but God is not a control freak, and he has given us our free will to choose him or not. If we choose not, then we will wind up in the slow cooker with the ones the place was originally designed for.

> Dear children, do not let anyone lead you astray. The one who does what is right is righteous, just as he is righteous. The one who does what is sinful is of the devil, because the devil has been sinning from the beginning. The reason the Son of God appeared was to destroy the devil's work. No one who is born of God will continue to sin, because God's seed remains in them; they cannot go on sinning, because they have been born of God. This is how we know who the children of God are and who the children of the devil are: Anyone who does not do what is right is not God's child, nor is anyone who does not have love for their brother and sister. (1 John 3:7–10 NIV)

Those who do not learn the teachings of Christ as God has given them to us in the Bible will be led down the wrong path by the devil quite easily through derogatory incitements referred to by biblically uninformed people as "fanatic religious zealots." Guess who these so-called religious fanatics are? They are the biblically informed students of the one true God, the God who made the rules whether we agree with them or not.

When a person who claims to be a Christian but who knows nothing of the true teachings of God calls a true believer a nut or worse…well, the proof is in the puddin'. So the next time you feel the urge to make fun of a person for his or her faith in the word of the Bible, you will actually be attacking a child of God. To paraphrase verse 10, "If you feel comfortable insulting your brother or sister, maybe he or she is not your brother or sister."

It is important to understand that when the Bible refers to brothers or sisters in the New Testament, it is not referring to blood relatives, at least not in the sense most people would acknowledge. The blood tie would be the blood of Jesus on the cross, and the relation would be brother and sister believers. Common blood siblings may not spend eternity with each other while the brother and sister who are linked by the way of faith will live forever under the wing of their shared Holy Father in heaven. If a child of God is not your sibling, you can't be a child of God, and that can only mean you are a child of the devil.

So you go to church on Sunday, but the rest of the week, you side with the knowledge provided by the devil. The Christian conservative really bugs you. Liberalism, and the ideas and ideals of mankind seem to be the real right way. These are pretty good indicators that you do not know the word of God. Satan has attached your pride to all his tools of deception.

By eliminating pride and opening your mind to the possibility of the Bible being the true route to salvation, you will loosen Satan's grip on you. When pride is defeated, all the tools of Satan will fall from the wall and crash to the ground, leaving the light of the Savior to guide you home. Nobody else needs to know. It is between you and your Creator.

Once a person leaves the darkness of evil, he or she can see the world for what it is. The light of truth will lead to a hunger for increased knowledge of the difference between good and evil. The issues that divide believers and nonbelievers are plainly visible in whom we choose to lead. Social issues are the realm of God. Satan employs the opposite of God. A true Christian is required to select leaders who subscribe to the teachings of Jesus.

The Bible is God's instruction manual. It is the only source of information that God intends the Christian to consult regarding social issues. To reject his teaching is to reject him. To reject him is to accept Satan. To accept Satan is to doom oneself to hell. Ignorance may not cast someone into oblivion, but it will prevent that person from achieving the necessary knowledge to make God-inspired decisions in all areas of life, including at the ballot box. So let's tackle the big issues as God views them and as Satan views them, from the only legitimate source available to all people: the Bible.

CHAPTER 3

Creation vs. Evolution
The Secret Superbowl of Good vs. Evil

> In the beginning God created the heavens and
> the earth.
>
> —(Genesis 1:1 NIV)

Perhaps when he willed the heavens and the earth into creation, God did it with a great big bang. Perhaps not.

The *NIV Life Application Study Bible* states, "The biblical view of creation is not in conflict with science; rather, it is in conflict with any worldview that starts without a Creator." The human idea of a big bang seems plausible. But what banged? What caused said bang? Could some sort of magic chemicals be responsible? How about magic beans? A flying moose? Maybe a flying squirrel and a talking moose. Can something be created from absolutely nothing? Wait a minute; absolutely nothing is something. It is absolutely nothing.

Let's try to get our minds around this. Imagine a completely empty room as the starting place for all existence. No, that won't work because there are still air molecules. We're going to need to suck everything out of that room to create a space filled with absolutely nothing, a vacuum. *The American Heritage Dictionary* describes a vacuum as "a state of emptiness; a void." Okay, that's done. We now have a completely empty room. But there are still walls; gotta get rid of those. Now we're getting somewhere. Oh wait; no, we're not because now we have no room.

The experiment requires we eliminate everything, including ourselves. For the experiment to prove anything, it must faithfully reproduce the beginning. This means eliminating everything, including us. There can be nothing to create the experiment. There can be nothing to conduct the experiment either because we don't exist, and neither does anything else.

Can something or anything come from nothing? The thought of it is ludicrous, every bit as fanciful as a talking moose. It takes far more faith not to believe in a Creator than to believe in a Creator. Yet, we have had leaders who deny a Creator in favor of something else, anything else. It does not take a whole lot of discernment to understand this is an open denial of God the Creator. So once again, we see the hands and feet performing the task of Satan.

Once we deny the Creator, we have eliminated God—and all his rules. Now that Satan has us eliminating God, evolution doesn't sound so farfetched. Since there is no Creator, evolution has to be the answer. We even see proof of evolution. Look at the variety of dogs that came from the first dog, the wolf. Yes, look at them. They are still dogs; they didn't become tigers or zebras. They are just dogs of different sizes, shapes, and colors. Kinda like people. Different sizes, shapes, and colors, but we are all still people.

To suggest evolution of man is to suggest multiple races. Since some dogs are smarter than others or may have different physical capabilities, the theory of evolution suggests they evolved to these variant capabilities. This would mean they are different species, but they are not different species. They are dogs.

By reasoning of the evolutionists, there should be superior human beings, those who evolved at a different rate than others. Bible-believing Christians believe God created a single human race in his likeness. Yet, is the Bible-believing Christians of the world the evolutionists are accusing of being racist. Who are the true racists? Those who reject the word of God and support evolution. Granted, some of these people don't realize they are rejecting God and favoring racism. That's the ploy of the devil.

An inherent characteristic of evolution is superior traits overwhelming unsuccessful traits. Since some humans evolved in the

Americas, others in Asia, and still others in Africa, Europe, the Arctic, and elsewhere, by evolutionary theory, some of us must be superior due to the evolutionary process being different to allow for our adaptive needs in various parts of the globe. Since the different races grew separate from one another, it only makes sense to the evolutionist that some evolved at a different rate than others.

If some of us are superior, then as thinking, rational human beings, we must, of course, find a way to assist nature in our continued evolution. If we are to survive, we need to eliminate the undesirables, such as the mentally handicapped and the physically handicapped, or at least prevent them from reproducing for the long-term development of humanity. The elimination of the gene pool of undesirables can only enhance our future.

Eliminating mentally disabled people was part of the Nazi plan of the 1930s and 1940s to eliminate an assortment of "undesirables." The bottom line of these efforts was to enable the "master race" to thrive. A master race is the end-game theory behind all evolution. There is really no need to spend much time addressing the evils of Nazism. Most people would agree the Nazis possessed little in the way of biblical values, although some non-Christians may prefer the term "family values" or "compassion."

Even members of today's far-left liberal faction claim to despise Nazism. When analyzing the political stance of today's left-wing supporters, their claims of disdain for the Nazis seem hypocritical as many of the ideals of Nazism are a hypothesis to the current liberal agenda. Many left-wingers desire that Down's Syndrome children be aborted, which would not only end the life of these tiny humans but would also safeguard the future of humanity by eliminating these faulty genes. Who will be the next victim of this gene purge?

As no human or group of people are capable of creating life from scratch, do we have any right to take it? Since we are not even capable of giving life to a single-cell amoeba, we are obviously out of our realm when we start making decisions about life and death. I will discuss government-mandated abortion in another chapter. For now, let it be sufficient that the idea of assisting evolution is just another way the devil has confused and blinded us to the ways of the master Creator.

It is time to truly rationalize the theory of evolution. According to Nicholas Bakalar's *New York Times* article dated June 19, 2015, a paper published in 2013 by Eva Bianconi of the University of Bologna in Italy says, a "standard human being" consists of 37.2 trillion cells.[8] That's 372 followed by eleven zeros: 3.72×10^{13}. That's a stupidly big number.

So in the beginning, there is a single cell that came from somewhere. This cell became a jelly-like gob of protoplasm. Eventually, this gooey mess became you and me. All thirty-seven-trillion-two-hundred-billion cells of us. Okay. Where is the link to prove we evolved from this single cell? Ahhh, the famous missing link is still being sought. There is actually no hard evidence of this single missing link. But should there be more than just one missing link?

Think of the process of human evolution as a standard three-hundred-page book. It all began at page 1. Today we are at page 300. What happened between page 1 and page 300? The whole book is missing, so we can only guess. Suppose we discover a missing page. Let's pretend it's page 150. We now know what occurred on page 150.

This, of course, is of no value in telling us what the book is about because without knowing what occurred in the previous 149 pages, we can only guess what is happening on page 150. We know nothing of the characters mentioned on the page, and we have zero knowledge of any character or plot occurrence not mentioned on the page. If we found about fifty more pages, we would have a better idea of what really developed. But the whole story would still be a semieducated guess.

As we evolved cell by cell, year by year, we finally became us. Since we know that humans haven't changed in at least six thousand years, it goes without saying that evolution takes a while. As each page of the three-hundred-page book provides evolution of the story, each new cell in the body provides evolution of the human. A new finger might grow at a microcentimeter every twenty-five thousand years. Gill slits may seal up at a centimeter every one hundred thousand years. Our tail disappeared gradually over ten million years. Centimeter by centimeter, that posterior appendage slowly vanished.

Since we have seen no change in the past 6,000 years, reason tells us that it must take at least 6,001 years for a single cell's worth of evolution to occur. That would place the time from page one to page three hundred at 6,001 × 37,200,000,000,000 years ago. So before we can validate the theory of evolution, we need to discover 37,200,000,000,000 × 6,001 missing links. So far, we have zero. We have not discovered one missing page from the story of evolution. There is absolutely zero evidence for evolution.

When a government mandates the elimination of a biblical view in favor of a contrary idea, that government is actually choosing to eradicate the biblical aspect. If the government allows the biblical and the antibiblical viewpoints to exist side by side, then the people of the nation retain the ability to choose, thus taking the government off the proverbial hook of damnation. When a leadership body chooses to side against the teaching of God, and the population does not reject that leadership, then the nation, state, county, or local municipality has rejected God in unison.

Many people, including self-professing Christians, have been led by the nose down a dangerous path. They have been prompted to believe that evolution is not a dangerous issue to side with. After all, lots of really smart science guys and gals seem to think it's okay. So are these smart folks smarter than God? Remember this: God makes all the rules. It's not okay to believe what we are comfortable with and dismiss the rest of God's teachings.

> By faith we understand that the universe was formed at God's command, so that what is seen was not made out of what was visible. (Hebrews 11:3 NIV)

There was nothing visible. No magic chemicals or magic beans. Nothing until the one true God who lives outside of time and existence as we understand it created it. When we start picking and choosing which teachings from God's word are worth paying attention to, we put ourselves in God's place. When we put ourselves in God's place, we become our own god, and presto, bingo—no God. Does the reader have any idea who jumps all over any opportunity to make God's children forget him? Creation is what the word of God teaches, and the lesson is all around us to see.

> The heavens declare the glory of God; the skies proclaim the work of his hands. Day after day they pour forth speech; night after night they reveal knowledge. They have no speech, they use no words; no sound is heard from them. Yet their voice goes out into all the earth, their words to the end of the world. (Psalm 19:1–4 NIV)

We see God's creation every day. We live in it every day. Our common sense tells us this didn't come from nothing. Still, some fall for the devil's deception and choose to believe a lie. Is it just an innocent little white lie that can do no harm? No! This little lie can lead us down a path that ends in destruction. When we correct God's word, we are correcting God.

> For God's wrath is revealed from heaven against all godlessness and unrighteousness of people who by their unrighteousness suppress the truth, since what can be known about God is evident among them, because God has shown it to them. For his invisible attributes, that is, His eternal power and divine nature, have been clearly seen since the creation of the world, being understood through what He has made. As a result, people are without excuse. (Romans 1:18–20 HCSB)

When our leaders determine that creation is not worthy of instruction in our schools, these leaders are deciding that God's way is not the answer. Clear and simply these government officials are saying the word of God is unnecessary. Some of these people may actually describe themselves as Christian.

People who describe themselves as Christian yet knowingly choose to disregard God's ways may not be saved. We certainly do not know for sure whether these people are saved, as we all, through the weakness of our flesh, consciously disobey the Lord from time to time. God can forgive these sins of the flesh if we are born of the Spirit and truly repentant from the heart.

There is a difference between the individual or government official sinning in private and his or her leading a group of followers to unbelief. When a nation selects to go the godless route, it is imparting hedonism on its people. Since the government is a political system of beliefs instilled by people, it is the people themselves who are responsible for their own hedonism. The government is not some nameless inanimate object to be blamed for the woes of its subjects, for it is the subjects themselves responsible for allowing their leaders' actions. In many cases, it is the subjects themselves who select godless leadership. When we choose godless leaders, those leaders will take the helm, and, if we allow them, they will steer us straight into the depths of depravity that only a society without God can understand.

If one thinks himself to be Christian yet selects a leadership administration that promotes godless institutions and ideals, the devil will drag the leadership and those responsible as far away from God as he can.

> For they knew God, they did not glorify him as God or show gratitude. Instead, their thinking became nonsense, and their senseless minds were darkened. Claiming to be wise, they became fools and exchanged the glory of the immortal God for images resembling mortal man, birds, four-footed animals, and reptiles. Therefore God delivered them over in the cravings of their hearts to sexual impurity, so that their bodies were degraded among themselves. They exchanged the truth of God for a lie, and worshiped and served some-

thing created instead of the Creator, who is praised
forever. Amen. (Romans 1:18–20 HCSB)

It is my most sincere desire that the reader consider the options
available in learning to cast a truly God-fearing ballot. The first and
by far the best thing to do is to pick up that Bible, blow the dust off
it, and open it.

How do you select a biblical political leader? The same way you
(hopefully) selected your pastor, minister, or priest. Think about it.
Why are you attending your current church? Do you like the music?
Maybe you prefer the old hymns. Perhaps you thrive on noninstru-
mental. Maybe you enjoy that everyone dresses to the hilt, or maybe
you go because it's just so casual. Did you choose to worship there
because it's just so darned accessible? I mean you can drive there in
three minutes or walk it in seven. Walk it? If they would just get rid
of that doggone traffic light, you could get home even quicker. How
could you not worship at this church? After all, so many of your
friends go there. Besides, they have the best coffee, and it's free.

All these reasons are something to consider. But should they
take first priority? To properly prioritize the reasons for attending
a particular church, it is easiest to eliminate the reasons you know
in your heart are pretty shabby. These would hopefully include the
free coffee, or the fifty-cent coffee, no matter how good it is. Dress
codes? Come on, really? Did Jesus require such a thing before he
would teach or heal? Just like art or humor, the music is a matter of
personal taste. If the music celebrates and honors the Lord, it's good.
If the type of music isn't exactly your cup of tea, it's something you
can get past.

Perhaps the second most important consideration before selecting a place of worship is the particular Bible version used at the
church. Some churches stand fast with the more staid approach of
the good old King James and feel that no other Bible should be read.
To these wonderful, loving Christians, as tenderly as I can, I remind
you that the original wasn't written in English at all. And again, with
as much love and concern for your feelings as I can muster up, what
about all the people of the world who don't speak English?

Remember the great commission of Matthew 28 and Mark 16:

> Then Jesus came to them and said, "All authority
> in heaven and on earth has been given to me.
> Therefore go and make disciples of all nations,
> baptizing them in the name of the Father and
> of the Son and of the Holy Spirit, and teaching
> them to obey everything I have commanded you.
> And surely I am with you always, to the very end
> of the age." (Matthew 28:18–20 NIV)

> He said to them, "Go into all the world and preach
> the gospel to all creation." (Mark 16:15 NIV)

Sure, we can verbally tell them. That is how much of the early testament was handed down from generation to generation. But we have an advantage. Through the Holy Spirit, we have God's truth in written form, a letter written directly to us from God himself. The Bible is the direct line to and from the Creator of the universe. Forget the Internet; we have the creatornet. He gave it to us, and he expects us to share it with everybody. How many people in the world will get any use from a Bible written in seventeenth-century king's English? Probably as many as read ancient Hebrew or Greek. We are to spread the word in whatever language it takes, not just ancient Hebrew, Greek, or old English.

There are those who enjoy the beauty of the 1611 English translation. To me, that's a personal-taste thing. I don't get it. With apologies to William Shakespeare, maybe I'm just not as appreciative as I should be of old English literature. To cut to the chase, pick a Bible that you understand. It doesn't need to be a study Bible, but there is nothing wrong with a study Bible. Just try to discern the word yourself without going to the notes too quickly. Allow the Spirit the chance to work on you. Life-application Bibles can be wonderful aids, and there are many available. As you mature in your faith, you will almost certainly want an assortment of Bibles. Although not an absolute necessity, it can be helpful to study the same Bible that your church uses.

The NIV is the most popular English language version at this time. But some scholars feel the New American Standard to be the most faithful translation. If you want to go old school but the King James is a bit intimidating, try the New King James, which is a reworked King James and sounds a bit more like the English we speak today. Don't get me wrong, the King James may be perfect for you. It just doesn't work for me. I guess some people are smarder den me is.

You can always get advice from your pastor. Get a Bible and read it. You can have a hundred Bibles and crosses in your house. You can have all the little fish decals you want on your car. Without a relationship with Christ, you have nothing. How do you form a relationship with anyone? By spending time with them. Pray and talk to God. There is no "correct" way to pray. If you're talking to God, you're doing it right. Your Bible is a cell phone signal straight to God, the Creator of the universe. This signal can never be lost.

What is the number one reason to select a church? Doctrine! If the teaching and preaching are pure biblical, you have found a church home. But how can you know it's biblically accurate? By reading your Bible. That's pretty simple, isn't it? By the time you have finished reading the five books of Moses in the Old Testament, you should realize the story of evolution is a great big fat lie being spread by the master deceiver, that filthy stinking liar Satan. Evolution is pure fantasy. We must not let Satan deceive us. His whole goal is to guide us down a path to a place without God. If there is no reason for a Creator, there is no reason for God. If there is no God, there is no need for Jesus. Without Jesus, we all perish; we all spend eternity in hell.

Every time one of us rejects God, the head coach of the other team has pulled a trick play that has resulted in a score against the great Creator. The desire of coach Satan is to drag us all away from the Savior. We must not fall for his trickery. We must keep our wits about us and use the knowledge of the holy word of God as our defense. The devil is a strong opponent, but he is no match for the Creator of the entire game.

Evolution? We must not believe the lie of Satan.

CHAPTER 4

The Final Solution for Israel Unwanted Prayer

The Lord had said to Abram, "Go from your country, your people and your father's household to the land I will show you. I will make you into a great nation, and I will bless you; I will make your name great, and you will be a blessing. I will bless those who bless you, and whoever curses you I will curse; and all the peoples on earth will be blessed through you." (Genesis 12:1–3 NIV)

Because of his great faith, Abram knew enough to obey a command from God. Even at the age of seventy-seven, he promptly packed up his wife Sarai, his nephew Lot, all their belongings, and all their people, and left Harran for the land of Canaan. When Abram reached Shechem, where the Canaanites resided, God spoke to him once again. The Lord appeared to Abram and said, "To your offspring I will give this land." (Genesis 12:7 NIV)

So why is the story of Abram worthy of a chapter in this writing? Because it is the covenant God made with Abram in the first book of the Bible. The first book written by Moses. The first book of the Hebrew Pentateuch (a book of five volumes). The first book of the

Septuagint (the Greek translation of the Hebrew Pentateuch). The first book of the Torah.

The covenant God made with Abram is the seed that grew into what we believe and are to live by today. It is from the bloodline of Abram that the Savior of the world would come. It was the descendants of Abram whom God chose to spread the word of the offer of salvation to the whole world.

When Abram obeyed God and left his country, his people, and his father's household to go to the land God would show him, he began a journey that would end with his name on a contract with God, a covenant with the Lord Almighty. God would make Abram's descendants into a great nation and a blessing with the task of spreading the word of Jesus to the entire planet.

Did Abram know of Jesus? Of course not. On second thought, yes, but not in the same way that we know Jesus. He simply followed orders from his Creator. He knew better than to disagree with the one responsible for all existence. He had a relationship with God and fathomed the Lord's great love for us. There is no way that Abram knew the plans of God, but he knew God himself and allowed God to use him, just as we need to do.

By forming a relationship with God, we will understand when he wants to use us for something. Abram did not know the long-term plans for him or his descendants. We don't know the long-term plans God has in store for us. We should, however, understand that if we ignore his plans for us, we are rejecting his intentions to use us for the greater good, which is always for his glory.

The great nation spoken of is the Hebrew nation. The descendants would be Jews. One of those Jews would be Jesus the Savior. Through Jesus, all believers are descendants. The blessing they would be is the hands and feet of God. God chose them to be his personal messengers to the world. God would give the New Covenant first to the Jews; then the Jews would give it to the Gentiles, meaning the rest of the world. God chose to use the Jews to bless the entire globe with the knowledge of God's gift of grace and salvation. Through the Hebrew nation, all nations would be blessed.

> Now there was a famine in the land, and Abram
> went down to Egypt to live there for a while because
> the famine was severe. (Genesis 12:10 NIV)

As it was the way of the Egyptian Pharaoh to keep any woman he wished as part of his harem, his people noticed the great beauty of Abram's wife, Sarai. Abram feared they would kill him and give her to Pharaoh. It was agreed that Abram and Sarai would pose as brother and sister. Indeed, Pharaoh took her and treated her "brother" well, giving him livestock and servants, but Abram and the Lord had a covenant in the works, and Sarai was to be an integral part of the deal. Even though Pharaoh was ignorant of the Lord's covenant with Abram, he and his people's lack of understanding was not to be an acceptable excuse. The world needed to be saved, and God's plan of redemption was not going to be thwarted so early on—or ever.

> But the Lord inflicted serious diseases on Pharaoh
> and his household because of Abram's wife Sarai.
> (Genesis 12:17 NIV)

When Pharaoh learned the real relationship of Abram and Sarai, he wasted no time in sending them packing. They were allowed to keep all of Pharaoh's gifts. God used this little episode of grief to give the bride and groom a nice belated wedding gift. Have a nice trip. Both Abram and Lot became wealthy, and at one point, there was just not enough grazing land for both of them in the same place as the Canaanites and Perizzites, who were also still around with their herds. Being close relatives, they decided it was better to split up than to bicker over grazing space. God used this, as well, to achieve his plan.

> The Lord said to Abram after Lot had parted
> from him, "Look around from where you are, to
> the north and south, to the east and west. All the

land that you see I will give to you and your offspring forever. I will make your offspring like the
dust of the earth, so that if anyone could count
the dust, then your offspring could be counted.
Go, walk through the length and breadth of the
land, for I am giving it to you." (Genesis 13:14–
17 NIV)

After they parted ways, Lot would settle in Sodom. During a
war between several rival kings, the city of Sodom was looted, and all
the goods and people were taken away, including Lot. When word of
Lot's capture reached Abram, he gathered the 318 trained warriors of
his household and went to rescue Lot. With God's blessing, Abram
defeated the allied kings of Kedorlaomer and released his nephew.
The liberated king of Sodom offered Abram all the retrieved riches
as thanks.

But Abram said to the king of Sodom, "With
raised hand I have sworn an oath to the Lord,
God Most High, Creator of heaven and earth,
that I will accept nothing belonging to you, not
even a thread or the strap of a sandal, so that you
will never be able to say, 'I made Abram rich.'"
(Genesis 14:22–24 NIV)

Abram would accept nothing but what came from God. The
king of Sodom was a Canaanite. Abram could not chance the possible future consideration of a debt to a Canaanite. The covenant
could now be written, and God spoke to Abram in a vision.

Do not be afraid, Abram. I am your shield, your
very great reward. (Genesis 15:1 NIV)

What was it that Abram could have been afraid of? If there was
any fear, it was probably the fear of the unknown. After all, he had
no children. How was God going to make his descendants a great

nation of numbers untold? It wasn't that he doubted God's ability to make it happen; he just couldn't figure out how. God didn't take long to provide the answer, as his word led Abram outside to do some stargazing.

> He took him outside and said, "Look up at the sky and count the stars—if indeed you can count them." Then he said to him, "So shall your off-spring be." Abram believed the Lord, and he credited it to him as righteousness. (Genesis 15:5–6 NIV)

You can bet that Abram was now pretty excited, but he still wondered, *How?* Well, what's the best way to garner a response to any mindful query? Ask! The nerve! How could Abram ask the Creator of all things, including life itself, what his plan was? Answer: would you not ask a loved one or friend about his or her intentions involving your future? You see, Abram had a working relationship with the true, all-loving God of the universe. Sometimes he may not see fit to provide an immediate response, but that doesn't mean he didn't hear the question or is ignoring you. God wants to hear from us. That's why he gave us his word in written form. The Bible and prayer are our cell phones to the Creator. All we need to do is talk to him. There is no secret method of contacting him revealed only after a lifetime of Bible study. He is ready and listening now and always. When we talk to him, that is prayer! Any thoughtful Bible study, alone or in groups, is prayer.

So Abram was just talking to his ready and willing heavenly Father. He asked in a straightforward manner how God was going to achieve this great accomplishment. God responded by drawing up a contract. He told Abram to bring a sacrifice, which would act as Abram's signature.

> So the Lord said to him, "Bring me a heifer, a goat and a ram, each three years old, along with a dove and a young pigeon." Abram brought all

> these to him, cut them in two and arranged the
> halves opposite each other; the birds, however, he
> did not cut in half. (Genesis 15:9–10 NIV)

In ancient times, the parties of an agreement would walk between the pieces of slaughtered animals to solidify a covenant. This symbolically linked them together and, at the same time, wished upon themselves similar destruction if they broke the deal. Remember the first time Pharaoh kicked some Hebrews out of Egypt? Abram and Sarai, the married couple, not the brother and sister, left with a boatload of treasure. Well, God told Abram it would happen again.

The Lord then came to Abram in a dream and told him of the four hundred years that his descendants would be the slaves of Egypt and the consequential punishment of their captors. He also told Abram of his descendants' eventual release, which would include great material possessions. Remember the first time Pharaoh kicked a Hebrew out of Egypt?

> When the sun had set and darkness had fallen, a
> smoking firepot with a blazing torch appeared and
> passed between the pieces. On that day the Lord
> made a covenant with Abram and said, "To your
> descendants I give this land, from the Wadi of Egypt
> to the great river, the Euphrates—the land of the
> Kenites, Kenizzites, Kadmonites, Hittites, Perizzites,
> Rephaites, Amorites, Canaanites, Girgashites and
> Jebusites." (Genesis 15:17–21 NIV)

So this is the land that God promised to Abram. But what about all these descendants? By now, Abram was ninety-nine years old, and Sarai was ninety. Maybe just a bit past childbearing age. A couple in their nineties having a baby? Impossible! Don't jump to conclusions. Remember what Jesus said in the gospel of Matthew.

> Truly I say to you, it is hard for a rich man to
> enter the kingdom of heaven. Again I say to you,

it is easier for a camel to go through the eye of a
needle, than for a rich man to enter the kingdom
of God. (Matthew 19:23–24 NASB)

It can be difficult for a rich man to deny his earthly wealth that
he can see and handle in favor of what is to him an invisible God.
At least that's what the devil tells him. His money does not convict
the man of means. He convicts himself by making monetary gain his
goal: his god. Money can be put to many good and righteous uses.
Satan, however, will use it to lure people away from God, and it is a
favorite tool of his. An idol is a replacement god. Any god other than
the one true God of Abram is false and only guarantees the believer
an eternity away from the real God. But!

"With God all things are possible." (Matthew
19:26 NASB)

Although most materially wealthy folks probably won't make
it, some undoubtedly will. After all, God never gives up on reaching
any of us. God can do anything, including figuratively drawing a rich
man through the eye of a needle. A ninety-year-old woman having a
baby? Piece of cake! That baby would be Isaac, who was the father of
Jacob, who was the father of Joseph and his brothers, and on and on
and on, until Jesus was born of Joseph and Mary.

So all the generations from Abraham to David are
fourteen generations; from David to the deportation to Babylon, fourteen generations; and from
the deportation to Babylon to the Messiah, fourteen generations. (Matthew 1:17 NASB)

No more talk. It was time to sign and notarize the deal. The
countdown to the arrival of the Savior had begun.

Abram fell face down, and God said to him, "As
for me, this is my covenant with you: You will be

the father of many nations. No longer will you be called Abram; your name will be Abraham, for I have made you a father of many nations. I will make you very fruitful; I will make nations of you, and kings will come from you. I will establish my covenant as an everlasting covenant between me and you and your descendants after you for the generations to come, to be your God and the God of your descendants after you. The whole land of Canaan, where you now reside as a foreigner, I will give as an everlasting possession to you and your descendants after you; and I will be their God." (Genesis 17:3–8 NIV)

God also said to Abraham, "As for Sarai your wife, you are no longer to call her Sarai; her name will be Sarah. I will bless her and will surely give you a son by her. I will bless her so that she will be the mother of nations; kings of peoples will come from her." (Genesis 17:15–16 NIV)

The next time you hear a self-identified Christian looking down on the Jews for killing Jesus, if you are a true Christian, you should know to correct that false Christian. A true Christian will absolutely be aware that the Jews are the people God chose to spread the light of truth to the rest of the world. The Messiah, the Savior of the world, was a Jew himself. A true new-creation Christian will know that we need to love the Jews and apologize to them for the great persecution inflicted on them through the ages in the name of Christianity. It is this historic hatred of the Jews by pretend-Christians that has resulted in their fear of the name of Jesus.

It is this misunderstanding of who Jesus is that keeps the Jews of today from recognizing that Jesus is the genuine Messiah they are waiting for. If someone told you that Jesus is the Savior of the world and then beat you and mocked you in his name, would you have any interest in learning more of him?

God used the Jews to spread the gift of salvation through faith in Jesus to the world. Now it is the world's turn to return the favor. For the Jews who missed the first coming, it is up to us to get them ready for the second coming.

It is also the Christian's obligation to support the Jews in their homeland. God gave them the land known as Israel. It is theirs. Any argument against this is a blatant disagreement with God. Those who claim the Bible is the inerrant word of God only when it is convenient need to show a little backbone; they need to be willing to take a little heat for their faith. We all stumble in weakness from time to time, but that should only serve as a warning that we need to strengthen our faith through prayer and Bible study.

Israel belongs to the Jews, and no human reasoning can change that fact. It belongs to the descendants of Abraham. God promised it to them. As believers in the one true God of Abraham, we are included as Abraham's descendants. If we side with Israel's enemies, we are not only rejecting the Israelites and God, but we are slitting our own throats.

We are a never-ending stream of broken promises and lies. God doesn't lie. God does not break his word. What if we try to take the Israelites' land away from them and succeed? That would make God a liar. It would mean he broke his covenant with Abraham. Do you think he will allow that? The nations surrounding Israel, as well as the rest of the world, can strike out at Israel all they want. They had just better expect failure. God is not going to let it happen.

> By faith Abraham, when called to go to a place he would later receive as his inheritance, obeyed and went, even though he did not know where he was going. By faith he made his home in the promised land like a stranger in a foreign country; he lived in tents, as did Isaac and Jacob, who were heirs with him of the same promise. For he was looking forward to the city with foundations, whose architect and builder is God. And by faith even Sarah, who was past childbearing age, was

enabled to bear children because she considered him faithful who had made the promise. And so from this one man, and he as good as dead, came descendants as numerous as stars in the sky and as countless as the sand on the seashore. (Hebrews 11:8–12 NIV)

Alrighty then. We see that God gave the land to the Hebrews. Let's get a good running start and jump ahead about six hundred years to get a more detailed vision of the exact borders of this land that God promised to the Hebrews. By this time, Abraham was long gone. His legitimate son Isaac had come and gone. His illegitimate son Ishmael had been born of Sarai's slave Hagar, and both had departed this life long before. Jacob and Esau had begun their everlasting rivalry, and both had passed away. The epic of Joseph had concluded 440 years earlier, but the long-term results of that story were only now wrapping up. The Jews had been freed from their four hundred years of bondage in Egypt. Their forty years of wandering was finally concluding. The Hebrews were at the threshold of the land of milk and honey promised them so long ago.

God was keeping his promise. But just like today, the Israelites had to earn his blessings. Today, a righteous person may pray for a better job. If it is within God's will and the person is not solely seeking riches for himself or herself, the person will find the job. But the new employer is not going to come knocking on the applicant's door. The job seeker must do his or her part. The job hunter must get up and go to work. It won't come free, but when following God's direction, he will expose the path to the job. He will be our roadmap due to our faith.

The promised land stood before the Jews, but first they needed to expel the wicked pagans who were occupying it. They needed to prove they trusted God by driving out the heathens. They had to get up and go to work. This type of work is not to be confused with works of righteousness. There is no work we can do to achieve salvation. When we believe in Jesus's death and resurrection, we understand the only way to eternity with the Lord is by his work. All we can do is repent from our hearts, confess with our mouths, and accept the gift of grace our Savior offers us.

When we are saved, we will want to do the right works. We will comprehend that these works of love cannot save us. These works of righteous love will include giving our resources and time to help those in need and to assist people in making the decision to come to the Lord. Righteous works differ from the work that comes out of faith that God will guide us to the place or occupation of his choosing to allow us to take part in glorifying him.

If the Hebrews truly believed that God was present with them, they would conquer their adversaries and receive the gift God promised them. They needed to listen and obey. If they didn't, they would pay the price. God would not break his promise to them; he would just find another way to build their faith that he was with them, and the prize was coming from him and not from their own efforts.

Like the wandering Hebrews, we must act without hindrance of disbelief. God's promise to them was no different than any promise he makes to us. If we have the faith and our wish is not selfish, but motivated by the love of the Holy Spirit, we will persevere.

God listens. God hears. With the Holy Spirit at our disposal, it is virtually unimaginable what we can accomplish. If we will only listen to his reply to our prayer requests and then follow his directives. Granting our desires will always be for his glory, yet it is always for our benefit.

Abraham listened and obeyed. God would now fulfill the promise, but action was still necessary. As we need to knock on the door of that employer if we're going to get that job, the Israelites needed to take action to get that promised land.

> On the plains of Moab by the Jordan across from Jericho the Lord said to Moses, "Speak to the Israelites and say to them: 'When you cross the Jordan into Canaan, drive out all the inhabitants of the land before you. Destroy all their carved images and their cast idols, and demolish all their high places. Take possession of the land and settle

in it, for I have given you the land to possess. Take possession of the land and settle in it, for I have given you the land to possess. Distribute the land by lot, according to your clans. To a larger group give a larger inheritance, and to a smaller group a smaller one. Whatever falls to them by lot will be theirs. Distribute it according to your ancestral tribes. But if you do not drive out the inhabitants of the land, those you allow to remain will become barbs in your eyes and thorns in your sides. They will give you trouble in the land where you live. And then I will do to you what I plan to do to them." (Numbers 33:50–56 NIV)

Did they listen and obey? They actually walked through a parted sea as one of a multitude of incredible signs of God's presence with them, so of course they jumped at the chance to demonstrate their obedience. Not! Their first objective was Kadesh Barnea, and they chickened out. But they walked through a parted sea! I'd like to think I would be one of the few exceptions to this act of disobedient cowardice. So did the apostle Peter, and he denied knowing Jesus Christ himself three times on Good Friday.

People are so weak, it's just plain stupid. We don't always fail our Lord, but when we do, we pay the consequences in this life. Those goofy Hebrews blew it. God would not break his word, but they had to pay the price. God gave them new marching orders. "About face; forward march! It's forty more in the desert for you!"

It just goes to reason that they swallowed their pride and obeyed orders. They turned around and walked away as instructed. Certainly not. They concluded that if they attacked on their own, this would appease God, and he would look the other way at their prior misjudgment. As the saying goes, "Two wrongs don't make a right." Without God at their side, they were horribly beaten. I mean they got spanked.

Moses warned them not to attack, but they did not listen. Now Moses gave them a big fat "I told you so."

> So I told you, but you would not listen. You rebelled against the Lord's command and in your arrogance you marched up into the hill country. The Amorites who lived in those hills came out against you; they chased you like a swarm of bees and beat you down from Seir all the way to Hormah. You came back and wept before the Lord, but he paid no attention to your weeping and turned a deaf ear to you. (Deuteronomy 1:43–45 NIV)

The moral of the story is we can always count on God to do what is best for us. Sometimes what's best is a little discipline. When a parent gives his or her kid a chore and the little one refuses, does the allowance still come? Most caring parents will withhold it or discipline the child in another way. The discipline doesn't come out of hate but from love. The ability to follow orders and complete assigned tasks is a stepping stone to humble submission. It is a lesson in respect, which will be an important attribute as the kid grows into early adulthood. As the kid matures, the learning opportunities will persist until the parents are gone. And then the learning continues.

The Israelites fouled up time and again, but their loving father in heaven did not stop loving them. He continued to teach them to follow the commands of the one who was blessing them as the chosen ones. They had a lot of growing up to do, and the current chore was driving the God-haters out of the land promised to them as the forebearers of all believers, the land God chose as his.

> Furthermore, we have had human fathers who corrected us, and we paid them respect. Shall we not much more readily be in subjection to the Father of spirits and live? For they indeed for a few days chastened us as seemed best to them,

but He for our profit, that we may be partakers
of His holiness. Now no chastening seems to be
joyful for the present, but painful; nevertheless,
afterward it yields the peaceable fruit of righteousness to those who have been trained by it.
(Hebrews 12:9–11 NKJV)

If we reject him and his discipline, we are running away and
telling Mom and Dad we hate them. This will break their hearts, and
they will try to convince us to come back. If we do not return, we are
lost. When we are lost in the dark and we attempt to lure our siblings
into the darkness, our parents have no choice but to save those other
children. They must prevent the black sheep of the family from dragging down the others.

So what of those poor Canaanites? God did not just toss them
out like rubbish. The Canaanites were idol worshippers. They had
totally rejected the true God, whose identity completely surrounded
them. As Paul so clearly states in Romans 1:20, "For since the creation of the world God's invisible qualities—his eternal power and
divine nature—have been clearly seen, being understood from what
has been made, so that people are without excuse." In other words,
it should be obvious to any dolt that a thinking entity created this
universe and all that is in it.

Paul followed up in Romans 2:14 when he said that God
inspired him to tell us the Creator placed in our souls the right way
to think (i.e., killing babies is bad, stealing is mean and selfish, etc.).
The one who created us wrote decency in our hearts. So his creation
is all around us to see, and he instilled in us the knowledge of good
and evil. God will judge based upon our knowledge and understanding. The Canaanites chose to reject these self-evident truths and to
embrace the wiles of Satan. God had to wipe clean of sin the land
he selected for his people. His precious gift to humanity must not
mingle with a corrupt society.

Many Americans today expect blessings from God because we
claim to be God-fearing Christians. "In God we trust" is even printed
on our money. If we are honest, however, we must admit that some-

times things from God may be a bit hard to swallow. It is steadfast obedience to God's rules and regulations that result in blessings, but it can be tough to be obedient. What we think God should approve of and what he actually approves of can be two separate things. If we condone sin in our land, the Holy Spirit will not attest to our virtue before God. In other words, we will not receive God's blessings if we make our own rules.

If the Israelites fell to the temptation to mix their true faith with the false beliefs of the pagan inhabitants, they could not reap the harvest of God's blessings. After all these centuries, the Jews found the big X on the map. This is the place. Did they wonder how much land belonged to them? They didn't have to. God gave them precise borders.

> The LORD said to Moses, "Command the Israelites and say to them: 'When you enter Canaan, the land that will be allotted to you as an inheritance is to have these boundaries:
>
> "'Your southern side will include some of the Desert of Zin along the border of Edom. Your southern boundary will start in the east from the southern end of the Dead Sea, cross south of Scorpion Pass, continue on to Zin and go south of Kadesh Barnea. Then it will go to Hazar Addar and over to Azmon, where it will turn, join the Wadi of Egypt and end at the Mediterranean Sea. "'Your western boundary will be the coast of the Mediterranean Sea. This will be your boundary on the west. "For your northern boundary, run a line from the Mediterranean Sea to Mount Hor and from Mount Hor to Lebo Hamath. Then the boundary will go to Zedad, continue to Ziphron and end at Hazar Enan. This will be your boundary on the north. "For your eastern boundary, run a line from Hazar Enan to Shepham. The boundary will go down from Shepham to Riblah on the

east side of Ain and continue along the slopes east
of the Sea of Galilee. Then the boundary will go
down along the Jordan and end at the Dead Sea.
"'This will be your land, with its boundaries on
every side.'" (Numbers 34:1–12 NIV)

So why is there a constant dispute regarding the borders of
modern Israel? The most convenient assertion is that all kinds of
people and religions exist in this world, meaning the Bible is not the
only authoritative source to determine such boundaries.

Many claim the nation of Israel is not a legitimate entity and,
therefore, has no business being in existence. One particular group
of people claim the Jews occupy a land that was originally inhabited
by a people known as Palestinians. There is truth in the statement;
however, there was never a bona fide nation of Palestine. Palestine is
a region, not a nation. Prior to being called Palestine, the area was
referred to as Philistia, which was the home of Goliath. Yes, that
Goliath, the Philistine large man David nailed with a stone. The
Philistines were a crude people, craving all things evil. God saw to
it that they fell at the hands of the Hebrews, and today there is no
ethnic trace of Philistines living.

The sixty-four-thousand-dollar question determining ownership of the land of Israel must be, what is Palestine and who are
the Palestinians? The *American Heritage Dictionary of the English
Language* offers this definition:

Pal-es-tine 1. The land between the Mediterranean sea and the
Jordan River that was occupied by the Hebrews in biblical times. 2.
This territory, occupied today by Israel.

As I have just pointed out, Palestine is a region or territory.
The word *Palestine* comes from the word *Philistia*, the name of the
area near the coast where the Philistines lived. The Hebrew name
for Palestine is *Israel*, or *Promised Land*. Jews and Arabs alike refer to
the land as Palestine, and the western portion of Jordan constitutes a
piece of the body of Palestine. Be aware that many Arabs claiming to
be of Palestine reside not only in Israel, but in Jordan, as well.

The so-called Palestinians are disparagingly candid about their desire to drive the Jews from what they consider to be Palestinian land. So why are they not also determined to evict the Jordanians? Part of Jordan actually rests on land God gave the Israelites in what was known as the Palestinian region of the Middle East, as is the case for Syria and Lebanon.

It is absolutely critical to understand that nobody owned Palestine before the Israelites. It was occupied by a people who despised God, but it was always reserved as private parking for believers and followers of the one true God. Granted, the Jews were kicked out a couple of times, but they were not permanently banned. They were punished for their sins of disbelief and disobedience; however, those God allowed to perform the eviction were eventually on the receiving end of God's wrath. These invaders of Israel were genuine God-haters being used for a worthwhile purpose.

In 586 BC, the Babylonians under King Nebuchadnezzar overran Jerusalem and brought the Jewish captives back to Babylon. For the first time in six hundred years, there was no nation the Jews could call home. It would be just forty-seven years until the Persians did in the Babylonians and released the Jews to return to their homeland. Cyrus, the king of Persia, returned all the booty the Babylonians claimed and urged the Israelites to rebuild their temple, which would be complete in 515 BC and stand until AD 70 when the Jews were once again forced to give up residence, just as Jesus foretold.

> Then Jesus went out and departed from the temple, and his disciples came up to show him the buildings of the temple. And Jesus said to them, "Do you not see all these things? Assuredly I say to you, not one stone shall be left here upon another, that shall not be thrown down." (Matthew 24:1–2 NKJV)

The Jews would finally come home again 1,878 years later. The homecoming party was held on May 14, 1948, when the State of Israel was established at the signing of the Israeli Declaration of

Independence. The following year, the United States and thirty-six other nations voted to admit Israel into the United Nations. Twelve nations voted no and nine abstained. The General Assembly of the United Nations required a two-thirds majority vote to admit Israel into the UN, and that requirement had been met. Israel is now officially recognized as a sovereign nation, even though God had recognized this many centuries earlier. So in biblical terms, as well as worldly terms (the United Nations ratification), Israel is the legal inhabitant of Palestine.

So what is the basis for so many people claiming Palestine to be an Arab holding illegally occupied by Israel? Jerusalem is spoken of throughout the Bible. The teaching in both the Old and New Testaments incessantly refers to Jerusalem as the residence of God and his family of believers. The Koran never once mentions Jerusalem, and the city has never once been an Arab capital, yet Muslims insist that Jerusalem is rightfully theirs. Much of the Muslim world claims they controlled Jerusalem first, so on this basis, it should belong to them. King David's conquest of Jerusalem in 996 BC predates the Muslim capture of the city by 2,500 years. Despite zero evidence to the contrary, Israel's local Mideast neighbors deny Israel's right to the land of their forefathers, the land the Jews claimed as their capital 2,500 years before the Muslims even arrived, the land God gave them.

It is plain to any subjective eye that there is no substantiation to the claims that someone other than Israel should hold title to Palestine. God chose the land to be the land of his people, and there is the answer to the next question: why are the Jews constantly persecuted?

The Jews have been relentlessly attacked throughout history. In fact, anyone who believes in the one true God of the Bible, Jew and Christian alike, are regularly scrutinized and held responsible for so many of the world's woes. A true believer understands that this persecution is born of the bowels of Satan. By convincing people of the political incorrectness of biblical Christianity, the devil hopes to halt the spread of the true word of God. God's chosen ones are, quite simply, disgusting to Satan. He hates the Jews and holds them responsible for his own future in hell. Satan goes out of his way to convince people that the Jews are nothing but sneaky, lying, greedy scoundrels, and those who don't trust in the biblical word of God succumb to his lies.

Even many self-professing Christians are fooled. If they kept God close through regular prayer and increased their knowledge through Bible study, these misguided people would step out of the darkness of Satan's deception into the light of God's truth. Israel belongs to the Jews, and in the future, to all true believers. Its boundaries are clearly marked. Jerusalem is its capital. To side against this is a grievous sin.

> I will make you a great nation;
> I will bless you
> And make your name great; And you shall be a blessing.
> I will bless those who bless you,
> And I will curse him who curses you;
> And in you all the families of the earth shall be blessed.
> (Genesis 12:2–3 NKJV)

"And you shall be a blessing," a blessing to the whole world since you will be used to spread the word of salvation through Christ. "I will bless those who bless you." If you praise them, God will take it as praising him, for if you praise them, you have faith and thanks in Him. "And I will curse him who curses you." Every nation or people who attacked the Jews has ultimately suffered defeat. Since 1948, the Jewish nation of Israel has been the recipient of onslaught after onslaught. Most of these invasions have been undertaken by armies of vastly superior numbers, yet the aggressors retreated with their tails between their legs every time, as Israel continues to stand strong.

This is not to suggest that the Israeli people are superior in some way to others, as they have been punished for sin digression in the past. But the promise God made to Abram all those centuries ago still stands. God doesn't forget, nor does he break his word.

If any nation on the globe stands against Israel or stands with its enemies, they are standing against the people God chose to use as the shipping company that delivered the Messiah. In other words, they are making a conscious decision to side against God. Even if it sounds like the right thing to do, even if it's the thing that will bring peace to the Middle East, even if it means Israel losing some of its God-given land, it is the wrong thing to do.

No peace is possible between God's family and Satan's. The only reason Israel's Arab neighbors claim Palestine as theirs is to eliminate God's people. If this were not true, then those so-called Palestinians would be receiving the loving care of their allies. But they receive nothing from their Arab allies, other than the urging to kill Jews and Christians in the name of their god, Allah.

Do not be fooled for a second. Allah and the God of Abraham, Isaac, and Jacob are not the same God. While the true God of Judeo-Christianity teaches love and forgiveness, Allah teaches death to the infidels. Do you really believe the same God worshiped in Christian churches and Jewish temples is the same god who orders some of his children to murder his other children?

Between 1948 and 1967, Jordan controlled the West Bank, and Egypt maintained authority over Gaza. Israel regained control over these areas in the six-day war of 1967. For nineteen years, Jordan and Egypt had the opportunity to peaceably surrender any of that land to create a new Palestinian state. They did not. No other Arab government even suggested the idea that Jordan or Egypt should give up any of this land to their brother "Palestinians."

The people claiming identity as Palestinians are Arabic people. Since Palestine is Israel and there was never a Palestinian state to begin with, these poor wandering souls are actually Jordanian or Egyptian. Rather than accepting these people with open arms, these two governments have chosen to use them as a cornerstone in their plan to drive out the Jews. Since the Jews are God's people, can't you hear the murmurs of Satan behind the scene?

The self-professed "Palestinians" would deny God themselves. In place of a life of peace living as a Jordanian or an Egyptian, they prefer to live a life dedicated to killing the hated Jew. Again, the stench of Satan lurking in the shadows is manifested. So do Israel's enemies desire a peaceful solution to the Israeli question? Most assuredly not. Israel's enemies are God's enemies. The only solution in their minds is the eradication of the Jews and the Christians, anyone who believes in the true Savior. The answer is not unwarranted violence but unwanted prayer. These enemies of God are no different than any born-again Christian. We too were destined for the brimstone and fire before we stepped into the light. God can soften the hearts of the wicked and show them the way exactly as he did for us.

But unabashed passiveness is not the obvious conclusion. Righteous self-defense is proper and expected. A preemptive strike against an enemy who is hell-bent on our obliteration is nothing more than an aggressive act of self-survival. Righteous anger is biblical and at times encouraged. So many people think of Jesus as this superwimpy sissy who just took it with a smile. The only thing he took was the punishment for our sins. He didn't necessarily smile when he was tortured and crucified. He suffered pain unimaginable to any human. He paid the penalty for trillions of sins committed by billions of people.

We need to remember that we are made in his image, which means anger is supposed to be present. Anger toward evil is righteous, but we have allowed Satan to bastardize the emotion. The devil uses anger as one of his tools to control us, and hatred of God is written all over this hatred for the people of God. Jesus did demonstrate righteous anger, and he was more loving than any of us could hope to be. Don't confuse loving kindness with passionate, righteous anger. Jesus illustrated this anger against sin on Tuesday morning of holy week.

> So they came to Jerusalem. Then Jesus went into the temple and began to drive out those who bought and sold in the temple, and overturned the tables of the money changers and the seats of those who sold doves. And he would not allow anyone to carry wares through the temple. Then he taught, saying to them, "Is it not written, '*My house will be called a house of prayer for all nations*'? But you have made it a 'den of thieves.'" (Mark 11:15–17 NKJV)

Adolph Hitler's final solution to the Jewish question was extermination. In the hearts of many today, that remains the answer. The real final solution in the minds of the followers of a godless faith is the elimination of any and all who believe in the one true God: Jews and Christians.

If you claim Christianity, yet side with the allies of Satan, you may be kidding yourself. You may be every bit as Christian as George Costanza was an architect. If you have flown on an airliner, this does not make you a pilot. If you have read a book, this does not make you an author. And just because it says "In God we trust" on our currency, that does not mean we trust in God or follow his commands. That does not mean we are a nation blessed by our obedience to the Lord...anymore.

> The day of the Lord is near for all nations. As you
> have done, it will be done to you; your deeds will
> return upon your own head. (Obadiah 15 NIV)

The answer to all questions is hovering around each of us all the time. God surrounds us. We are engulfed in his presence. By opening the Bible, anyone who asserts to be a believer in Christ will become enlightened by the truth. This truth can only lead to a closer, more knowledgeable relationship with the Lord. Jesus said that to those who don't believe, this would all be foolishness. Is it foolishness to you? This is a bunch of nonsense to the enemies of God. The enemies of Israel. The enemies of Jerusalem. The enemies of Zion.

God hears righteous prayer and responds to it. Righteous prayer from true believers that the unsaved will listen and accept the everlasting peace that comes from the only source it can—the one true Creator of heaven and earth—is the one thing that can lead to peace in the Mideast and the world.

This is the final solution in the heart of God—that everybody will choose Him. We have our free will, for God is not a dictator. He is a loving Father who dearly wants us to choose to come home to him. Our prayer for the unbelievers who delight in the destruction of Israel is that God might soften their hearts and they might come to the Savior. Our prayer is that all unbelievers might become new creations in the warm glow of God. Our prayer is that all might recognize the Christ. This is the final solution most dreaded by the devil. To Satan, this is the most unwanted prayer.

CHAPTER 5

Abortion
Only Jesus Can Free Us

Picture in your mind the last time you saw a tiny newborn in the arms of his or her mother. Remember the innocence of the child? Recall the helplessness of the baby? The little child had a bearing of sweetness that wasn't marred by the gurgling, the drooling, the burp, or even that unmistakable scent of baby poo.

With no apologies whatsoever, when the discussion veers toward abortion, it is obligatory at the commencement of the exchange of thoughts that the topic of discussion is human life. It is arbitrary whether one believes in God or not. It makes no difference if I am prochoice and you are prolife. With respect to any point of view, the subject matter when discussing abortion is human life. The disagreement may be about when life starts or who has more rights, the mother or the child? The question may be when is a fetus considered an independent human being? Regardless of any view, the subject matter is human life. Is it alive or isn't it? If it isn't alive, then a fetus has no more rights than a corpse. Does a corpse have more rights to civil protection than a living person? In any type of dignified disposal, the dead body does take certain precedence over the living person.

Some cultures prefer the remains of loved ones be cremated. Some ancient societies who believed in mythical gods would burn the body to ensure the smoke would carry the soul of the deceased into some type of promised land or heaven.

In our own contemporary western society, many feel cremation is disrespectful to the body of their loved one. With the rising costs of a complete burial service, however, more people are considering cremation as a more cost-effective method of disposal.

While the ancient Egyptians buried their Pharaohs with all their earthly belongings, this is generally not done today. The Egyptians were misguided, to say the least. Pharaoh was looked at as a god who was capable of taking along all his earthly possessions. Few from any nation, culture, or religion, however, subscribe to this belief today.

The Christian and the atheist alike are devoid of any difference of opinion on the subject of the need to pack up a dead person's belongings and bring them along at the funeral. All people are pretty much in agreement that a dead body is void of all feelings and memories. It is dead. It has less use than a chair or a bicycle. If kept around, that cadaver will decompose and become a health hazard, not to mention a nightmare to the individual who stumbles on it and then turns to see what caused the misstep.

So at the end of physical life, our worldly bodies become useless sacks of rotting flesh and organs. Should there be laws to ensure a proper and respectful elimination of Aunt Edna's body? There is nothing wrong with safeguarding ourselves from the spread of disease. On this count, it is absolutely the prudent thing to do. Aunt Edna's family loved and cherished her presence and will miss her very much. To provide her earthly remains with a respectful burial is something many people feel is all they have left to give her. It is a way to say good-bye in a manner of esteem.

Even the Bible-believing Christian, who may have a fairly good idea of Aunt Edna's eternal destination, will on occasion visit the place of her remains. Sometimes we just want to give our passed away relatives a hug, and since we can't take the bus to heaven, we just go to the place we feel will bring us a little closer to them. Sometimes it can be soothing; other times not. In any case, it does not bring them back into their bodies. But to those who read and understand the teachings of the Bible, it is only a matter of time when we will be together again. Hopefully, that reunion will be in the clouds with the Lord.

The next time you feel the need to visit a long-gone loved one, find a nice comfortable spot and open the word of God, our Savior. Delving into the warm light of the Bible will usually wash away those feelings of guilt, sadness, or loneliness.

In fact, whenever the devil assaults you with feelings of hopelessness, grief, or remorse, just put the attack and those feelings in God's hands. God is always there for us. My pastor once conducted a series of sermons he titled "Jesus Frees Us." The lectures greatly helped me understand that when the devil attacks me with feelings of inadequacy as far as my faith is concerned, I need to put it in Jesus's hands. He will free me from the grip and temptation of Satan.

When a person we love dies, it hurts. Even if we are true believers, we will still feel the pain that comes from the longing to see that person again. We feel sad at the death of anyone, even strangers, because as much as we will miss a lost loved one, we are aware that the stranger will suffer the feeling we all understand so well.

For the true Christian, the feeling of loss can be magnified when we believe that person never accepted the gift of grace. But God can also relieve our pain when we understand if we believe and understand that we are going to see that person again, and the next life will never include separation. This gives us hope and drives a need to thank our Creator for being so understanding of our needs.

So when we are born-again, our spirit will never really become a useless lump of dead tissue. We will live forever. The question is where will we spend eternity, in heaven or hell? Sorry, but there are no other choices. There is no place in between. The fence-straddling occurs here, in this life. At death, we will all fall one way or the other, but we make the entire decision for ourselves whether to lean outside the kingdom or inside. God is calling us from the inside while the devil is summoning us from the outside.

Not simply a Bible-believing, but a Bible-educated Christian should have a grasp of all this. Being Bible-educated does not mean possessing a degree from a great seminary. While scholarly Bible teachers are of vast importance in guiding us in understanding certain idiosyncrasies of the Bible, through their knowledge and understanding that "Jesus frees us," nothing is quite as satisfying as the enlightenment that comes from receiving our own revelation from God.

It is important to understand the entire truth of life and death to better enable us to comprehend the whole abortion conundrum. As we have seen, our spiritual selves will not end. They will continue after our bodies perish. But are our clumps of rotting flesh gone forever?

> And after my skin is destroyed, this I know, That in my flesh I shall see God. (Job 19:26 NKJV)

We will spend eternity in our new and improved bodies, which means we will recognize and know each other. It will be a glorious reunion. The prophets of the Old Testament concluded our bodies will be resurrected, and our spirits will rejoin them.

> Your dead shall live; Together with my dead body they shall arise. Awake and sing, you who dwell in the dust; For your dew is like the dew of herbs, And the earth shall cast out the dead. (Isaiah 26:19 NIV)

> There will be a time of distress such has not happened from the beginning of nations until then. But at that time your people—everyone whose name is found written in the book—will be delivered. Multitudes who sleep in the dust of the earth will awake: some to everlasting life, others to shame and everlasting contempt. (Daniel 12:1–2 NIV)

These are the same prophets who were 100 percent accurate when they foretold the first coming of Christ 500 to 1,400 years in advance and were flawless down to the last detail. Can there be much greater evidence of the godly inspiration behind their predictions? Did

I say predictions? That's kids' stuff reserved for Las Vegas odds-makers. The stuff of the Bible is supernatural, truly God-inspired.

It is these same God-inspired folks of the Old Testament who foretold the first and second coming of Christ. And that's not all. The Lord let them in on a whole bundle of other goodies, including the prophecies I just related from Job, Isaiah, and Daniel. I could present additional Old Testament examples, but it is my hope that this is enough to get the point across that we will be rejoined to our bodies at some point. Don't worry; God made us from scratch, and he knows how many hairs each of us has, and how many pores are in our skin. Even if a body was cremated and spread over the Atlantic Ocean, God will have no trouble piecing it all back together. So in case you are wondering, no, it does not matter how our bodies are disposed of after death. It's all good.

In the last line from the book of Daniel, the Lord sums up the whole story with these words:

> As for you, go your way till the end. You will rest,
> and then at the end of the days you will rise to receive
> your allotted inheritance. (Daniel 12:13 NIV)

The Jews still believed in the accuracy of these prophecies during the time of Jesus's first coming, 500 to 1,400 years after the prophets wrote them. When Jesus came to raise Lazarus from the dead, he told Lazarus's sister:

> "Your brother will rise again." Martha answered,
> "I know he will rise again in the resurrection at
> the last day." Jesus said to her, "I am the resur-
> rection and the life. The one who believes in me
> will live, even though they die; and whoever lives
> by believing in me will never die. Do you believe
> this?" "Yes Lord," she replied, "I believe that you
> are the Messiah, the Son of God, who is to come
> into the world." (John 11:23–27 NIV)

Jesus himself taught of the physical bodily resurrection in the end-times.

> For as the Father has life in himself, so he has granted the Son also to have life in himself. And he has given him authority to judge because he is the Son of Man. Do not be amazed at this, for a time is coming when all who are in their graves will hear his voice and come out—those who have done what is good will rise to live, and those who have done what is evil will rise to be condemned. (John 5:26–29 NIV)

The people have acted either out of faith or a lack of faith. Their actions didn't save them, for only by the grace of God through the blood of Christ can our sins be washed away and our purity assured.

So the followers of Jesus believed in the bodily resurrection, and all the things he taught, which had been prophesied earlier. Can you guess who didn't believe? The Sadducees did not believe in the end-times resurrection and, like the Pharisees, missed the obvious link between Jesus and the Christ; as foretold by the same prophets, these big-shot Jewish religious leaders read and studied regularly. Their eyes were wide open, but they were blind to the truth. This should serve as a stringent reminder to study the word for ourselves. We need to open the Bible and learn, so we won't be deceived and end up in hell. Only through open-minded studiousness can we make the correct choice.

Political correctness can at times sound nice and may seem like the right thing to follow, but remember, God makes the rules. Don't be blind to the truth. The subject of this discussion is life, and we have seen that it goes on endlessly, in heaven or in hell. It is our choice. That pretty much sums up the end. But what about the beginning?

> Then the Lord God formed a man from the dust of the ground and breathed into his nostrils the breath of life, and the man became a living being. (Genesis 2:7 NIV)

That sure would be the beginning. I'm talkin' "THE BEGINNING"!

You may be wondering, *What has the creation of Adam have to do with abortion?* My response is, "Pardon me?" After creating Adam, God created and gave life to Eve. Obviously, he did not stop there. He has created several billion people, and he ain't done yet. Here comes another, and now another, and here's one more. The births just keep steamrolling along, little boys and little girls of the next generation. These little ones are not only children; they are grandchildren, great grandchildren, great great grandchildren, and...you get the idea.

These tiny babies not only have a connection to the past; they also have a connection to the future. One day they will be parents. After that they may become grandparents, then great grandparents, and so on.

God's creation of Adam was really the creation of all of us. When Adam and Eve sinned in the Garden, they sinned on behalf of us all. When Christ died on the cross, he died for us all.

Keyword: All!

Adam and Eve's sin was our sin. We are all born with the sin of disobedience. Only one was born unbestowed of sin. We are all of the one Creator. Only one was the Creator. We are all blessed with God-given life. Only one can give life.

Only God can create. Humans can make things but not create them. Man can make all sorts of machines, some mechanically operated and others digitally driven, but man makes these inventions from the raw materials created by God. No human being will ever have the capability to create rocks, dirt, oil, coal, trees, or minerals. Man is not able to create electricity, only to harness it. The power of electricity comes courtesy of its Creator.

Through the prophet Isaiah, the Lord advised the Hebrews:

> It is I who made the earth and created mankind
> on it. My own hands stretched out the heavens; I
> marshaled their starry hosts. (Isaiah 45:12 NIV)

If a human being is unable to create a stone, why would he or she think himself or herself capable of creating a flower, a mouse, or another human being? Crossbred flowers are made from preexisting flowers. Cloned mice are made from the cells of a preexisting, God-made mouse.

God created human life and gave us the freedom to use it as we choose, but only we have the right to decide the final outcome of our own lives. It is most assuredly our responsibility to nurture our young, to guide them down the path that leads to their decision to follow Christ. We are to meet their physical needs when they are too young to care for themselves. When they mature to the point they can interpret right and wrong, they can decide their spiritual outcome independent of us. Their lives are universally their own.

It is not up to anyone else to determine the outcome of another individual's eternal destiny. When we take the life of another, we deny that person the opportunity to honor his or her loving Creator by choosing him. Childbirth is the way we multiply our numbers for the Lord. The Messiah himself came into the world in the normal manner, although the conception was a tad out of the ordinary. I wonder what would have become of us had Mary aborted the baby Jesus because she didn't think Joseph would have understood. That, of course, is pointless speculation and maybe even a sin of doubt on my part. God knew what he was doing and selected the right people to take part in the greatest case of childbirth in history.

When John the Baptist was six months old, he was aware of his surroundings. He was not yet out of the womb, yet he had a sufficient connection to the outside world to know there was an important visitor at hand. When Mary went to visit Elizabeth, John reacted with the same joy that infused his mother.

> When Elizabeth heard Mary's greeting, the baby leaped in her womb, and Elizabeth was filled with the Holy Spirit. (Luke 1:41 NIV)

> As soon as the sound of your greeting reached my ears, the baby in my womb leaped for joy. (Luke 1:44 NIV)

John the Baptist was aware of the outside world three months prior to birth. King David understood that awareness commenced even earlier than that. We are aware the moment we are conceived. Our physical bodies grow around who we are. We exist and possess the sin of Adam and Eve before we are born into the world.

> Surely I was sinful at birth, sinful from the time my mother conceived me. Yet you desired faithfulness even in the womb; you taught me wisdom in that secret place. (Psalm 51:5–6 NIV)

God expects a Christian of reasonable faith maturity to have enough influence from the Holy Spirit to make righteous decisions regarding biblical teaching. When a born-again Christian, through ignorance of the truth, comes to a faulty conclusion, this could be considered sinful. None of us has all knowledge, and if anyone claims to be all-knowing, that person is most definitely on the wrong path. Only one is all-knowing, and that one is not you or me.

A sin committed out of ignorance is not the unforgivable blasphemy. Like any other sin, it can be washed away. But if a person persists in spreading a lie of the devil, even out of ignorance, then that person is allowing himself or herself to be used by Satan to spread deceit. When we support a civic leader who adheres to nonbiblical standards, we are as responsible as the candidate we support.

It is our Christian responsibility to educate ourselves of God's standards and then to see how they compare with our candidates for public office. The life/choice issue is clouded by secular thought, which is always a plumb line to deception. For the true Christian, there is no choice. The light of truth bathes the issue in certainty.

> My frame was not hidden from you when I was made in the secret place, when I was woven together in the depths of the earth. Your eyes saw my unformed body; all the days ordained for me were written in your book before one of them came to be. (Psalm 139:15–16 NIV)

The Bible makes it clear that the Lord knows us before he places us in our bodies.

> The word of the Lord came to me, saying, "Before I formed you in the womb I knew you, before you were born I set you apart; I appointed you as a prophet to the nations." (Jeremiah 1:4–5 NIV)

Before God tells the stork to deliver us, God knits us together in the womb. The moment the first stitch is placed, which is the exact millisecond of conception, we are God's living children. We are human. At that instant, God assigns us our future tasks of glorifying our Father in heaven. All we need to do is physically grow and then accept the truth that enables us to step into the light of the Savior.

The great trifecta of lies perpetrated by the proabortion assemblage is that most abortions are required to spare the life of the mother, that a fetus is not living matter, and that it is a woman's choice whether to give birth to her child. According to studies completed by the Guttmacher Institute in 1987 and 2004, only 3–4 percent of all abortions are carried out due to the mother's own concern for her health, not necessarily the concern of medical professionals.[9] Rape and incest combined to form an almost insignificant number of reasons for abortion.

Almost all abortions are committed for social reasons (i.e., "I can't afford a kid now"; "I don't want anyone to know I'm having sex"; "A baby will get in the way of my career"). Only about one half of one percent cite rape or incest as reasons for abortion. These statistics are also supported by studies from the Guttmacher Institute as cited in Andrew Wommack's book *Christian Philosophy.*[10]

The fetus is not living? At just twenty-two days, the baby's heart is pumping his or her own blood, quite often a separate blood type from the mother.[11] The third great lie, the one about it being the choice of the mother, is in reality the weakest argument the abortion promoters can employ.

As we have just seen, the word of God tells us we existed in the body and heart of God before conception, which is the moment we are living human beings.

You shall not murder. (Exodus 20:13 NIV)

This is the sixth of the Ten Commandments. The command does not continue. The directive includes no addendum providing for the exception of the murder of one's own child. It contains four words, and four words only: "You shall not murder." Many women have had the procedure performed out of ignorance because of the lies they've heard from the abortion industry. They may have fallen for Satan's horrible deception that a fetus is not alive and feels nothing. Perhaps the abortion was performed prior to the woman being reborn into the family of Christ.

Sadly, there are women who might be genuine born-again Christians who just didn't find the time to mature in their Christianity. If they had only prayed about their decisions or immersed themselves in the word and teachings of God. He gave us the Holy Bible for a reason. Answers to all questions are included between its covers. If they had only known.

Ignorance is not an excuse for abortion, just as it is not an excuse for any other sin. But when the realization comes that sin has stained our lives, the Holy Spirit will convict our hearts. The pain we suffer when the Holy Spirit reveals our sin to us is small potatoes compared to the pain God feels when we permanently reject him. He will forgive! If he can forgive us, we should be able to forgive ourselves.

It may sound corny and almost serve to trivialize the pain we suffer upon realizing our own sin, but it is true that what's done is done. We can't go back in time. We can only deal with it the best way possible, which is to put it in his hands. Jesus frees us from all pain and despair. I have occasionally felt pain and hopelessness, just like anybody else. When I put those feelings in Jesus's hands, however, miracles have happened.

As I am a man, I cannot fully understand the anguish a woman must undergo once she realizes abortion is sin. But I can sympathize, to a certain degree, what it must feel like to kill, whether purposely or accidentally. I was never a soldier, but I can still feel concern for the traumatized warrior who killed for his country. The resulting horrors from combat are reserved for those who endured it. My point is, although we do not all suffer the same bone-jarring grief, we all suffer grief. Sometimes the detriment can be more destructive than anyone else could ever imagine. But whatever the pain is, Jesus can heal it.

Someone once confronted me with the argument that it is not right to bring up abortion because I never know when someone present may be struggling with the guilt of a past procedure. I related to this individual an occurrence from my past, which at first seemed somewhat uncaring and noncomparable to post-abortion trauma. Once I finished telling the story, however, I hoped it would drive home the truth of Jesus's ability to heal all wounds. The story I related was not a creation from my imagination. It was and is the truth.

My mother passed from this life in August 2013. She was a lifelong Catholic, and all three of her kids attended Catholic school. I was the youngest of the three and the only one to attend kindergarten. Upon graduation from grammar school, I followed my sister and brother to a private high school. Then it was off to the altered world of college.

On the outside, this sounds like a pretty good start. Truth be told, I wasn't the greatest student. Nonetheless, I would have thought my knowledge of the Savior would have been a bit more than it was after all those years of parochial school and Sunday masses. Oh, I knew all the Old Testament stories, but they were nothing more than adventure tales. I still did not recognize the value of Christ. The story of the passion was just another tale that meant nothing to me.

Leap ahead to the early 1990s. I was operating a private business that included a nineteen-year-old salesman who just happened to be a born-again Christian. Business went South, however, along with the girl I intended to marry. Mom started to act funky. Her memory was fading, and she was pretty confused. That Christian employee started telling me about Jesus, but my listening was half-hearted because I thought I had heard all those stories. I had never read the Bible, but the nuns told me all about it. So in my mind, I had nothing new to learn, despite this young man's persistence in telling me about it.

After some months, I came to the realization that I was asking questions, some of which I was sure were coming out of left field to this poor kid with Jesus in his heart. At Christmas, I was dumbfounded when he presented me with my very own Bible. I was now able to look up answers on my own. But it wasn't until I finished reading the four gospels that I accepted the gift and became a new creation, even though I hadn't yet finished reading the entire Bible. It took some time before the foul language and humor faded, and the greed, drinking, and smoking were eliminated. But my personal revelation had occurred. I understood that in my past life, I was rowing down a river that was getting hotter and hotter. Jesus held his hand out, I grabbed it, and he pulled me out of that boat to hell.

My hunger for the word grew the more I learned. My personal symbol of greed, my little company, was gone. Mom was continuing to decline and was now officially diagnosed with Alzheimer disease. With the business down the drain, I took a job driving a passenger van for a ground transportation airport shuttle company. The money was adequate but not eye-popping. My Bible was my constant companion even though some days it would not be opened.

As it turned out, I was a true believer, yet my relationship with God wasn't growing at an alarming rate. I read my Bible but not with the passion that leads to great things. I was still ignorant of things a true Christian should know.

By the time my employment at the shuttle company reached a couple of years, I had been saved for about four years. I was still not really growing, however, due to my sporadic Bible study. I needed to mature, and God knew just what to do to light my fire. Back-to-back major plumbing disasters at the house, and an assortment of unexpected financial issues were breaking the bank. Then came the blow that would eventually put it all together. My car was stolen with my Bible aboard. While taking the train home from work, two armed robbers picked me clean.

At the same time, Mom's physical and mental health were declining. The number of prescriptions to be filled was on the upswing. We were now at the point where a caregiver needed to be brought in while I was at work. My siblings and I agreed that unless it was absolutely essential to make a change, it would be better for her to remain in the familiar surroundings of her home.

Due to the need to get home in order to allow the caregiver to leave, my overtime at work was severely limited. But I was gonna get through this on my own. I was fully aware of God, but it was as though I lived on the East Coast and the Lord on the West Coast. If I could find the time, I would shoot off a quick e-mail to God. I managed to buy another car, but not another Bible. My relationship with him was becoming a thing of the past. While I was busy trying to work things out on my own, and firing off that quick message to God, I completely missed him pounding on the door and yelling at the top of his lungs. My Savior was trying to reach me, and I wasn't listening.

My self-inflicted infection of stupidity was growing into a big swollen, pus-filled whitehead of grief. The electrician I brought in to take care of a little problem found something else, something dangerous, something in need of immediate repair. Did I mention that at this time the mail presented me with the gift of a traffic ticket, and my credit card company let me know that someone just used my card to purchase $800 worth of liquor?

The electrician needed exactly two hundred bucks the next day. I didn't have it. My selfish pride prevented me from asking my sister or brother for help. Mom was in a wheelchair, so the thought of a fire was mind-numbingly terrifying. I told the electrician to do the work. I would figure out how to pay him later. The following morning, I went to work as usual. I went through the motions, but my heart was not in it. I felt drained. I could control nothing. No matter how hard I tried, everything around me was failing. I doubted my ability to continue to care for Mom. The day dragged but eventually came to a close.

As I pulled up to the hotel to drop off the last passenger of the day, I was not looking forward to going home. I loved my mom and would normally look forward to seeing her smile at recognizing me, but I felt I was letting her and everyone else down.

God would use the final passenger of that wearisome workday to transform my life. I learned beyond a doubt that a saved person can slide back and not lose salvation. The passenger was a man of about fifty. He was tall and of average build. He bore no facial hair and wore no glasses. He brought with him a single, medium-sized tan piece of luggage. It was well-used and included a few scuff marks. The bag was not filled completely and seemed to hold enough for a short stay.

As I handed him his bag, I wished him a good stay as I do to all my passengers, but I knew there was little sincerity in my tone that afternoon. I could barely complete my indifferent wish of a happy stay when this man asked; "Do you believe in God?" Without hesitation, I responded, "Yes, I do." As he handed me a roll of cash, he told me, "This is for you." He walked toward the hotel entrance as I quickly glanced at the amount of money he had given. Immediately, I felt the tug of righteousness. I felt unworthy of this money as I didn't feel I had earned it.

I thought, *Quickly, before he gets away, give it back.* I called out to him and said, "I can't take this." He responded without a moment of thought, "Yes you can! It's yours!" At this, I told him the truth. "I don't know what to say." The man knew I did know what to say, and he told me so. "Yes, you do!" I said, "Thank you, God." The man smiled from ear to ear and walked into the hotel. I returned to the driver's seat in the van and counted the cash. Exactly $200. Just what the electrician needed.

Something went through me so instantaneously that I have trouble describing it. I say it was the only time in my life that I heard the voice of God. It was not my mind's voice. It came from without and from within at the same time, and it was only two words: "Remember me." In that instant, I saw how many times I missed his attempts to reach me. I saw and felt his joy at my coming home to him. I felt his laughter as he kidded with me about my stubborn do-it-myself attitude. I thanked him for not giving up on me.

That night, I began to pray again. My relationship with our heavenly Father took on a new urgency in my life. And—I bought myself a new Bible. Only now I made opening it daily a most irredeemable mandate. It didn't take long before cultivating my relationship with God and preparing myself for his use became the most important things in my life (with his guidance, of course).

As my faith matured, he gave me more opportunities to serve through spreading his word, primarily in one-on-one encounters, with increasing complexity as I grew. If God is going to use me in any grander scale, I have no clue about it. One of my personal struggles is impatience, and I have this all-American need to spread the word quickly. Right now, we need to get everybody saved. Right now! God knows my capabilities and uses me suitably. If there is one thing I have learned, it is that both the simple questions and the hard questions require the same answer: the Gospel.

Never get sidetracked. Don't get sucked into a secular discussion. These are the deceptive techniques of the devil. He cannot defeat the word of God, and he will use every slippery method in his book of lies to take our focus off the Gospel. I finally heard the calling to come home. As my faith grew, the problems seemed to dissipate. On a regular basis, I began to share the word of God with Mom. As I have already alluded to, she was a Catholic in good standing. Her loving and concerned ways were evidence of her bearing the Holy Spirit.

I, on the other hand, never committed to the Lord while I was a Catholic. With no injustice to the many true God-fearing Catholics who may read this, I feared for my mom's salvation due to my own nonacceptance as a Catholic. The more time we shared reading the

Bible, the more I began to realize that she may be a child of God, but I had to be sure. A true believer does have the gift, to a certain extent, to recognize a person who is in need of the truth. Only through studying the word, and by the blessing of the Holy Spirit, can we get a feel for who may be in danger of cooking in the oven. It was a nineteen-year-old kid who saw my skin getting toasty. He perceived my need for salvation because he had already been saved, and the Spirit had blessed him with the ability to recognize my need.

I had to be sure about my mom, so I prayed to the Lord. It was apparent that her time on earth was nearing completion. I asked God to give me a sign. I needed to be sure that when she died, God was bringing her home to him. Her cognitive powers had fallen off dramatically. Her memories were fading as fast as her physical capabilities. The simplest mental exercises were becoming a challenge. When asked to name three animals, three colors, or three cities, she sometimes rattled off three in a heartbeat. The next day was a success if she even opened her mouth. On many days, two plus three was too much for her.

As the end neared, a recognizing stare was about the best to be hoped for. Through my tears, I continued to ask for a sign that she would be with her Savior. "Please, God. Please, Jesus. Don't take her if you can't assure me that she is going to you." I pleaded with God to give her the time to decide.

Then it happened. On a particularly bad day for her, she recited the Lord's prayer without a hitch. It was then that I realized she was able to ask the occasional question only when I read to her from the Bible. The absent gaze would dissipate when we read from the word of God. The Holy Spirit resided in her. I knew she would go a place with no more pain. She would no longer be in a place where her loving son would occasionally lose patience. That son must live with that until his own passing. But he is content that she is in a better place. As that son, I can only ease my guilt by giving it to the Lord. He can forgive this as he can forgive anything. We all suffer guilt from some transgression in our past. Only Jesus can free us. He knows our weak flesh, and he accepts true repentance in his name.

On the day of her passing, I was at her bedside in the hospital. The Lord gave us time to say goodbye. Something told me to close the door to her room. I pulled the chair I had been sitting in most of the day even closer to her. Though she was unconscious, I told her, "Mom, just you, me, and Jesus are gonna spend some time together." I began reading to her from 1 Peter. About twenty minutes passed when I noticed her breathing getting strange, and I called the nurse. In a matter of moments, the crash cart was in the room, but it was over. The last line of scripture read in that room was

> For you were like sheep going astray, but now you have returned to the Shepherd and Overseer of your souls. (1 Peter 2:25 NIV)

I didn't ask for a second sign, but God gave it anyhow. Jesus was with us in that hospital room, and he knew the pain I would feel. He knew my need and offered himself to me. It could only be Jesus who would free me from the pain of such a loss. There was no doubt of my mom's presence with the Lord, yet I still struggled with the loss. I wondered what I was doing wrong. God had assured me of Mom's nearness to him, yet I couldn't shake off the hurt.

There came a point where I started to feel shame for grieving so selfishly. I missed her and wanted her back, yet I fully fathomed the plain fact that she experienced more love and joy in her first minute with Jesus than I could have provided in ten lifetimes. I continued to arrogantly pray for God to remove the pain. I was ashamed of myself. *It's all about me*, I thought. *If I am really happy for Mom, I should not be this depressed.* The prayers continued to flow for God to take away the grief, but as incessant as the stream of prayers were streams of tears. I thought, *Perhaps I'm finally experiencing the agony I should have felt when she was alive and suffering.* It was now getting confusing, and I didn't know where to turn. I never got angry with the Lord. Instead, I thanked him for bringing her home. In my contorted, twisted logic, I even managed to overthink this. I began to wonder if I was thanking God for bringing her home or if I was thanking him for informing me. *Is this still all about me?* I wondered.

During her last weeks at home, Mom slept in an electric hospital bed in her bedroom. Every night before helping her into bed, we would sit on the bedside together and share a prayer. After tucking her in for the night, I would give her a kiss and a reassurance of my love for her. There was nothing that meant more to her than a hug and a kiss from one of her kids. The doors to her room were French style, and one would be left open a bit to allow me to peek in without disturbing her.

After her passing, I would still go in there to say a prayer before I retired for the night. I knew this had to stop sometime, but it just seemed the time had not yet arrived. The prayers for relief persisted.

The old house that had been in the family for more than sixty years was going to have to be sold. My sister, my brother, and I knew of no other place for our childhood memories. They never informed me, but I suspect they understood that as I was the one who cared for her until she passed away, I should be the one to decide when it would be time to move on, let the past go, and continue living.

The emotional turmoil assaulting me was getting harder instead of easier. I truly was not sure what to pray for. Finally, I stopped trying to rationalize it all. As I lay in bed one night, I felt a sudden anger. I don't really know what was ticking me off. I just felt powerless, and my anger exploded. I raged at the devil, at God, at life, and at the world. I knew with all my heart that I really didn't hate God for letting my torture linger, though I do believe God allowed me to wallow in my anguish long enough until I was prepared to fully place it at his feet. I cried for God to extinguish my anguish. He did so in a dream.

In this dream, he allowed me to see my mom. She would not speak to me, and there was not a hint of heaven visible. But he allowed her to visit me. I was walking with her along a sidewalk in the city. She was still the ninety-year-old, five-foot-tall woman that she was when she left. But she was walking and holding my hand.

When a man approached us from the rear, we stepped aside to allow him to pass, as we were moving along at a relaxed rate. As the man passed by, suddenly Mom pulled her hand from mine, and she ran across the grass parkway, over the curb, into the street, and surged ahead of the gentleman while I ran behind her, pleading for her to be careful. She jumped the curb, crossed the grass, and let me catch her ten feet ahead of the man we had let by. I laughed as I told her not to do such a thing as she could fall. Once again, we permitted the man to pass.

Our stroll continued, and I couldn't help but to notice her sly little smile. In just a short time, we came across a parking lot enclosed in chain link with a single pedestrian gate hanging open. The parking lot was immersed in a thin layer of water no more than an inch deep. This water glistened like a sheet of fine polished glass.

Mom shrewdly lulled me into a state of unreadiness. It was preposterous to consider that she would again break free of me and run like an Olympian. She had to be aware of the danger involved in a repeated stunt of springing about. She was ninety years of age, not ten. She saw that inch of water and took off like a bird out of heaven. I pursued, but had no chance of catching her. As I watched in horror, imagining broken bones and lots of hospital time, she performed a swan dive into the single inch of water. The awful thud I expected did not happen. Instead, she glided like a cartoon character across the water, arms and legs elevated above as she glided along the surface. When she came to a halt, my pursuit continued. I frantically splashed to her side, and she rolled on her back to greet my late arrival. The smile on her face, the color in her face, the light in her eyes were more than I saw in her when she was alive on earth.

She held her hands up to me. As I reached forward to help her up, in an instant, I was transported back to the French doors of her bedroom. Instead of her warm hands, I gripped the door handles. Slowly and frightfully I pushed the doors open and looked to the left. There sat my mom on her hospital bed, waiting for me to take my customary spot next to her for our nightly prayer. After I took my place next to her and looked her in the face, tears came from me, but they should have come from her. She was miserable in a way I hadn't seen before.

When she was alive, I could think only of keeping her here, even when my patience wore thin. As I was viewing her at this point, however, she was pale, lifeless, and tired. Her eyes were dry of tears, but it was only because she knew they wouldn't ease her agony. I couldn't conceal my grief and reached with both arms to hold her. I would not get to touch her as I woke from the dream at that moment.

Even though I knew beyond a shadow of a doubt that Mom was in heaven, my sense of loss was overwhelming, and Jesus came to help. He illuminated to me in a physical way how much better off she is now.

The next time someone tells you that your departed loved one is in a better place, don't take it as a well-meaning quip from someone who just doesn't have the words to express their concern. If that loved one was a true believer, that little quip is a mountain of truth.

I can never thank God enough for blessing me so many times with his unique medicine for my grief. I'm not certain why he granted me the gift of seeing my mom in her glorified state. Other true believers have not received such a blessing, yet God permitted me to view my mom after her death in a body that could only perform the things she did in a supernatural state. I saw her in a state of joy that can only be described as unearthly spiritual splendor. And he let me revisit her agony at the end of this life, further glorifying her eternal existence with Jesus.

The only reason I surmise that I received this gift of emotional healing was not that I somehow better petitioned the Lord than other true believers; on the contrary, my weakness of faith may have required a more obvious answer to my prayer. Regardless, it was Jesus who freed me from my pain, and he can heal all pain.

A person who has had an abortion or who has performed abortions can be freed as well. Jesus knows we hurt, and he feels the pain with us. He wants us to come to him in our times of need as well as in our times of happiness. He not only wants to celebrate victory alongside us, but he also wants to be there in our times of suffering. He knows our flesh is weak, and we make critical blunders from time to time. But no pain is too deep for him to render harmless.

No matter what anyone has done, if repentance comes from the depth of the heart, Jesus can heal it. We must never be hesitant to give this truth to a person who needs to hear it. I have no doubt I will be reunited with my mom as well as other true believing family members when I leave this life. I can only pray that all my earthly family and friends will one day become my heavenly brothers and sisters. It is the only way we will remain together forever.

Sometimes it can be better not to see a loved one again on this earth if our own faith serves only to drive them further from the truth. Sometimes, the closest ones in this life also misunderstand us the most. We must remember, they know us best. They know our faults. They remember when we lied or displayed unrighteous anger. In their sight, we can teach them nothing. In these cases, it is best to avoid a wedge-driving confrontation and pray for God to put someone in their lives they might listen to.

God can heal all wounds. People can be in need of healing and not even comprehend the need due to a lack of self-worth, guilt, a terrible thought, or plain ol' anger. Through prayer to my Savior, I have received healing from anger, jealousy, grief, worthlessness, and even smoking. I was a cigarette smoker for thirty years and quit with no help from any expert or program. It was the strength of the Holy Spirit inside me that led to my victory over tobacco addiction.

Since I also enjoyed a beer or ten every now and again when I gave up the cancer sticks, I needed to relinquish the alcohol habit as well. As any smoker will readily testify, a beer can't be had without a cigarette. Only through my avowed recognition of the prodding of the Spirit was I able to obliterate two detrimental practices in one mighty swipe.

A true believer should want such power over personal detractors. Belief without growth will abandon even the true Christian to a life absent of the blessings of the Holy Spirit. A limp, half-hearted search for the truth and influence of the Spirit will culminate in a half-truth instilled by the whole devil. Only by studying God's word can we really mature in faith to a point where the devil can only shake his head and say to himself "Man oh man, that's another one who got away."

It is my hope the reader will understand that my life has been one long chain of events dictated by Jesus as victory over everlasting damnation and clear dominance over evil in this life. The battle will continue as long as I live. In his hatred of God, Satan will assault me every chance he gets. Only through my faith, knowledge, and under-standing of the mastery of God over Satan will I continue to defeat the devil and be free of his wicked manifestations.

Only one method can drive out the devil's insufferable attacks. God the Father came to this world as one of us to teach us "the way" and to pay our sin debt through his death, to defeat death through his resurrection, and to remain with us as his surrogate through the Spirit. Victory comes from the Holy Spirit, who is Jesus, who is God. The Holy Spirit leads and teaches exactly as Jesus taught. To speak to the Spirit is to speak to Jesus.

Only Jesus can free us of all our anguish. But don't take my word for it. Read the word and find out for yourself. Then you too will realize the same miracles that Jesus has bestowed on me and millions of believers.

Read your Bible and give Jesus the chance to free you too.

CHAPTER 6

Marriage
The Rules are Clear and Simple

Traditional marriage is under assault by the liberal left spearheaded by the Democratic Party, which largely recognizes the homosexual community at the expense of the heterosexual majority. We must remember that the attack is targeting the biggest supporters of traditional marriage, the membership of the church who recognize marriage through the eyes of God, the marriage taught by God as being between one man and one woman.

Many, if not most, of the traditional Republican Party look the other way on this subject, becoming metaphorical allies of the left. Lack of opposition to an issue is recognition and acceptance of the issue. For this reason, Bible-believing Christians view with skepticism both major political parties in America in the early twenty-first century.

While the Bible does not state that marriage is strictly to be between a man and a woman, time and time again it mentions homosexuality among the long list of the violations of marriage. So, can two men or two women be married in the eyes of the Creator of marriage? Unless a person is so absolutely convinced that a believer in God's teaching must be trashed at any expense, it is obvious that by the regulations stated in the Bible, marriage is limited to the participation of only one man and one woman.

So is a Christian to be castigated for believing in the teachings of the Bible? In the eyes of the nonbeliever, any Christian is to be persecuted without mercy simply for believing something contrary to the belief system of the unbeliever.

The nonbeliever will readily accuse the follower of God's word of being narrow-minded and hateful. In other words, nonbelievers will always label Christians intolerant of their ways. While intolerant haters of our faith consistently and viciously attack us, their repetitious banter rings in the ears of the godless media, who in turn release a barrage of mindless and baseless charges on our beliefs, no matter what the subject might be. Marriage may be one of the hot topics today, but tomorrow it may be abortion, and the next day it could be public worship.

We should try to remember, as hard as it may be, that these people who hate and ridicule us are exact replicas of ourselves before we stepped into the light of God's grace. The object of their anger is not us personally but who we represent in the eye of their master.

The master of deception, Satan himself, has fooled these people. As Satan cares nothing for us and is obsessed with hating God, those he rules over are attacking God. It is God, his rules, and his children the devil is attacking. It is God who is being assailed. We are just standing in the way. So as Christians, we need to be resilient to the assaults from the devil's unwary supporters. God is requiring us to speak the truth no matter the outcome. Remember, we are not really doing the talking; we are allowing the Lord to use us.

> But when they arrest you, do not worry about what to say or how to say it. At that time you will be given what to say, for it will not be you speaking, but the Spirit of your Father speaking through you. (Matthew 10:19 NIV)

> But make up your mind not to worry beforehand how you will defend yourselves. For I will give you words and wisdom that none of your adversaries will be able to resist or contradict. You will be betrayed even by parents, brothers and sisters, relatives and friends, and they will put some of

> you to death. Everyone will hate you because of
> me. But not a hair of your head will perish. Stand
> firm, and you will win life. (Luke 21:14–19 NIV)

In the previous passage, the Lord was speaking of what will happen to believers in the end-times, which began at Jesus's resurrection. From that moment, the devil has been leading a barrage of attacks against believers. Christians and Jews have been relentlessly bombarded due to their belief in the one true God since the beginning.

While it is true that Satan will increase his rage as the end comes closer, it is his end that will be coming, and he knows it. This is why the intolerance of the world against believers is on the increase. Satan is nearing his end and he is pushing his army of unbelievers to wage a war of relentless persecution against God's children. It matters not at all to the true believer, and we should all be aware that even the most ruthless persecution can never really harm us.

> I tell you, my friends, do not be afraid of those
> who kill the body and after that can do no more.
> But I will show you whom you should fear: Fear
> him who, after your body has been killed, has
> authority to throw you into hell. Yes, I tell you,
> fear him. (Luke 12:4–6 NIV)

To properly let the Holy Spirit of the Lord function through us, we need to allow him in by opening ourselves to the teachings of the Bible. We access our better understanding through prayer and meditation in the word. What the uninformed and immature Christian understands of the sacrament of marriage can be the same as the unbeliever because neither usually studies the Bible. Even the newborn Christian is generally biblically ignorant until such time occurs that increased knowledge leads to enough growth to comprehend on a larger scale.

Since we are in a state of constant and eternal growth, it is not for the Christian to look down on or criticize a fellow believer. It is, however, the duty of the more mature believer to nurture the less mature. There will always be someone with a greater depth of understanding than I, and I am grateful to that person for his or her patience with my lack of maturity in his or her eyes. Thus, I must exercise patience with those less informed than myself.

Those who have come into the family of Christ have become new creations in him. We have been born a second time, but if we do not grow in our faith, we will remain helpless babies unable to discern for ourselves right from wrong. Someone will always be trying to lead us down their true path while we readily accept it, not knowing if it is the real "right way."

When we were born to our earthly mom and dad, we were dependent on them for everything. Slowly we grew and began school. In the blink of an eye, we went from starting kindergarten to graduating from the eighth grade. On we went to high school and then to a trade school, college, the military, or straight into the workforce. Every step of the way, we learned something new. It started with the alphabet and never stopped. Even people who didn't complete elementary school continue to learn and grow through life experience.

A person who is born again but who refuses to grow is almost like a baby who refuses to leave the womb. The baby who will not grow has ended his or her own life. Since it is impossible to live and not grow, the newly born Christian has effectively self-aborted. To live and not grow is to live in a state of self-imposed vegetation.

So the Christian view of marriage is that it is a joining of one man and one woman. While heterosexual sin is no more grievous than homosexual sin, since God can forgive both, claiming any sin is not sin is the blatant correction of God, which idolizes oneself as being more worthy than God to make the rules. This is replacing the real God with oneself, thereby rejecting God's authority, which is the unforgivable sin of blasphemy.

What the uninformed believer or nonbeliever does not grasp is that when the Christian stands against homosexual marriage, the point of dispute is not the homosexuality. Rather, it is the marriage that is the main concern.

> Then the Lord God made a woman from the rib he
> had taken out of the man, and he brought her to the

man. The man said, "This is now bone of my bones and flesh of my flesh; she shall be called woman, for she was taken out of man." That is why a man leaves his father and mother and is united to his wife, and they become one flesh. (Genesis 2:22–24 NIV)

The reason they become one flesh is to become a new family and give birth to offspring. Two men or two women cannot become one flesh, as they are incapable of bearing offspring, thereby becoming a new family. Jesus confirmed this in the gospel of Matthew.

"Haven't you read," he replied, "that at the beginning the creator made them 'male and female,' and said, 'for this reason a man will leave his father and mother and be united to his wife, and the two will become one flesh'? So they are no longer two, but one flesh. Therefore what God has joined together, let no one separate." (Matthew 19:4–6 NIV)

When Jesus returns to us, he will be coming to get his bride, the church. It is not the Methodist Church, the Lutheran Church, the Catholic Church, or the Presbyterian Church, but the family of believers, the one true church, not the church around the corner from my house or the church you attend on Sunday, as there are certain to be some false believers at these.

The true church may include people who hold the truth near their hearts and understand and repent of their sin, who will be judged on their acceptance of the knowledge presented to them. Some of these folks may have never even had the opportunity to attend an organized worship service, but if they are repentant believers, they are part of the one church. They are the bride of Jesus.

Has not the one God made you? You belong to him in body and spirit. And what does the one God seek? Godly offspring. (Malachi 2:15 NIV)

As a spouse belongs to his or her partner in marriage, we belong to our Savior. We are to be faithful to God, just as we are to be faithful to our marriage partner. When we choose to idolize something else, it is the same as choosing someone else. As most would agree, choosing someone else while married is adultery.

When someone chooses to wed in homosexuality, this is selecting to disobey God and create another love: the love of sin. The earthly adulterer is easy to define, and a lengthy description of adultery is not beneficial to the lesson of spiritual adultery. Spiritual adultery is replacing Jesus with another belief.

Some may suggest that in this modern world, there is no longer room for all this Bible hobo jobo. The Bible was fine in its time, but we have moved beyond the need for such primitive ideas. In this world of freedom of choice, we should have the freedom to choose which gender we wish to be, plumbing be damned.

God has not changed in all of eternity, which is a pretty good indication that his laws have not changed either. Are we so evolved and advanced that we have become God? The human body has not evolved, and neither have our abilities. Despite what the science fiction movies offer, there are no human beings running around with oversized craniums and the ability to think objects across the room. God has not changed, and neither have we.

Biblical truth does not change; only the lessons taught by the misguided change. The truth is the truth, and no teacher of falsehoods can alter that fact. Some of us were taught the truths of the Bible at an early age, and over time the taunts and temptations from the other side influenced a change in our thinking. We chose to cheat on God by shacking up with an idea that sounded more fun at the time. Others were not presented with the truth, and the enemy has obstructed the path to the truth at every opportunity.

Whatever the case, we choose our destiny. The fact remains that the truth of old remains the truth of today.

> Jesus Christ is the same yesterday and today and
> forever. (Hebrews 13:8 NIV)

While polygamy existed in the Old Testament and was even practiced by some God-loving individuals, it always led to friction and often shame. Polygamy is another form of false worship. It is symbolic of a person having more than one god in a universe where there is only one God. Monogamy is taught as the ideal. Polygamy, on the other hand, is a form of adultery, and adultery is forbidden with no exceptions.

> You shall not commit adultery. (Exodus 20:14 NIV)

This age of sexual freedom has made it fine and dandy to present a loved spouse with one of the greatest pains in life, the pain caused by a cheating husband or wife. This devil-may-care attitude toward sexual fidelity crops up because we feel the teachings of the Bible are out of date!

That grief in the victimized spouse is a result of a society inundated by sexual freedom without consequences. Sorry, but there are always consequences to all our decisions.

> The acts of the flesh are obvious: sexual immorality, impurity and debauchery; idolatry and witchcraft; hatred, discord jealousy, fits of rage, selfish ambition, dissensions, factions and envy; drunkenness, orgies, and the like. I warn you, as I did before, that those who live like this will not inherit the kingdom of God. (Galatians 5:19–21 NIV)

> Do not be deceived: Neither the sexually immoral nor idolaters nor adulterers nor men who have sex with men nor thieves nor the greedy nor drunkards nor slanderers nor swindlers will inherit the kingdom of God. (1 Corinthians 6:9–10 NIV)

The scripture does not add that if you feel it's okay, then God will look the other way on some of these issues. Some people might see this scripture as being kind of harsh. The only proper response to that opinion is: grow up and deal with it; the truth is not always easy to accept.

Your parents disciplined you the best way they knew how. It sometimes stung at the time, but later in life, you realized they were quite often right. They were not always right because they were not Mr. and Mrs. God. They did the best they could to raise their young.

> Know then in your heart that a man disciplines his son, so the Lord your God disciplines you. Observe the commands of the Lord your God, walking in obedience to him and revering him. (Deuteronomy 8:5–6 NIV)

Our parents were no different from any of us, and they were no different from their parents. They were sinners who were destined for eternity away from God unless they were born again. While we are all doomed to hell because of sin, some, admittedly, are a bit more obvious in their desegregation. Some are so vile as to be recognized even by the unsaved as destined for hell. But we are all eligible for Jesus to clean and polish us and make us right with God.

> And that is what some of you were. But you were washed, you were sanctified, you were justified in the name of the Lord Jesus Christ and by the Spirit of our God. (1 Corinthians 6:11 NIV)

While many recognize John Wayne Gacy, Adolph Hitler, Al Capone, Saddam Hussein, and Osama bin Laden as being remarkably bad people, only the saved, who are occupied by the Holy Spirit, can see the evil in the rest of humanity. No, we are not all good deep down. The truth is just the opposite, and the word of God confirms this. Just open your Bible to learn the truth.

We are all really good? That's just another lie from Satan to steer us away from the Good Book. Again, I must state that the devil will do whatever it takes to keep our noses out of the Bible. Once we know the truth and accept it, Satan has lost us.

Homosexual marriage is a hot topic today that has been around for a long, long time. Any form of assault on the truth has been around since Satan tempted those two in the Garden of Eden. All the evil and lies of the devil have been going around in an endless circle for ages. Just ask those residents of a couple of towns called Sodom and Gomorrah.

Considering how touchy this subject is, one might expect this chapter to be among the longest in this book. But homosexual marriage is really as simple to address as this: God makes the rules, and God says homosexuality is a sin and a violation of marriage. God presented the rules to us, and a true forgiven believer understands that we didn't, don't, won't, and can't make new rules. End of story, and end of chapter.

The homosexual sinner and the heterosexual sinner are alike. When either decides a particular decree of God needs updating, it is likely that the person is struggling with a sin that is defeating them. Perhaps deep down inside, the sinner knows the sin activity he or she can't stop is wrong, so the person decides God must be wrong in that particular case.

Of course, God is not wrong, and we are just tired of fighting him, so we create an excuse to continue in that particular sin. The problem with doing that is we are caving in to the taunts of the devil. Once we fail to resist the temptation, we fall under Satan's influence, and he will easily convince us to adamantly reject any person who comes toting scripture. In no time Satan will have us accusing believers of being narrow-minded haters of all who disagree with the Bible. The truth is we were deceived, and the devil has us justifying our sin.

The devil will never convict our hearts with the only way to get out of the sin trap he led us into. He has weaved his web of lies for ages and will do anything he needs to prevent us from listening to the true teachings of the Master Creator.

While we may struggle with our sin, no matter what it is, only the love of Jesus can free us from the torment of the devil. One of my own weaknesses is a lack of patience, which can lead to anger. Over my years as a born-again believer, this problem has subsided, but it still remains something I struggle with. Your sin may be kleptomania, lying, pride, gluttony, same-sex attraction, or something else. Putting it in the hands of the one who constantly tempts you to repeat the sin is not the answer. All he will do is try to convince you that the one who can help you is full of beans.

The truth is the truth. It is just that simple. God makes the rules, the Holy Spirit will convict our hearts (guilt), and Jesus will be our defense attorney. If we are really sorry and truly believe in the death and resurrection, God will know it and deliver us from our just punishment. Any time we make an excuse to justify our sin, we reject the true teaching of the Master Educator.

No matter how difficult the struggle, Jesus can aid in our effort to defeat our sin hang-up. All we need to do is give the problem to him and listen for his direction. But we absolutely must remember that our sin does not have to be of any concern to him. He does not have to do anything to help us; yet, he will always do everything he can to rescue us from sin because of his never-ending love for us.

Wouldn't it be a whole lot easier to admit that he is the teacher, we are the students, and he decides who graduates to an eternity with him? Those who fail the class do not get a retake. This is it. But the Lord has provided the answers in writing. Life is the easiest class any of us will ever take. The teacher has given us all the answers. All we need to do is accept them.

CHAPTER 7

To the Unbeliever and the Deceived We, Too, Once Did Not Believe

The task of addressing lies that appear to be the truth can be a daunting undertaking for one simple reason: these lies appear to be the truth! That is the whole idea. A lie that seems to be the truth will not be questioned. Why should it be of any concern? After all, it seems to be the truth.

A trained military sniper is taught to remain concealed. The sniper may blend in perfectly with his surroundings. His target might look directly at him and see nothing more than some bushes and trees. The victim sees what appears to be a lot of shrubbery. For the most part, what he sees is true. Those trees and bushes are truly there. But something else is present among the truth. Something that is not right. Something that is a lie. A lie concealed as the truth. The lie is a sniper so well-camouflaged as to blend in perfectly with the trees and shrubs.

The target sees 99 percent truth. He accepts the landscape as innocent and harmless. If he was to study that landscape, however, he might see something out of place. He might notice a movement not normally associated with branches blowing in the breeze. He might recognize a clump of leaves bearing an abnormal resemblance to a human head and shoulder. He may pick out a stick so straight that it could only be manmade. Perhaps the stick is really a rifle barrel.

In a moment, with no warning, the sniper squeezes the trigger, and the intended victim becomes the consummate victim. A single lie hidden among the truth became the deadly truth for the victimized target. This is the way of the great deceiver, Satan. He will borrow the truth to use as camouflage for his lies. The devil is the one who ultimately fires the shot, but he needs a trigger on his weapon. When we fall for his lie, we become the weapon, trigger and all. He uses us to spread his lies and destroy others.

Satan can use human leaders of nations, businesses, and even churches as weapons of mass destruction. If the evil one can convince a church head, an industrialist, or a national president that the ways of Satan are the ways of Jesus, then Satan can use that human leader to guide the masses down the road to oblivion.

The bureaucrat becomes the gun, and the underlings and followers become the targets if they choose to mindlessly follow along. The people don't have to follow, however. They can look into the bushes and trees for themselves. They do not have to take the word of a leader. God has given them eyes to see and ears to hear. They can search for the truth themselves.

The forest is the truth the sniper used to conceal himself. The Bible is the truth of God, and Jesus desires that we look at it. If we do not read the word of God, we are blinding ourselves. We are not using the eyes God gave us to study the forest. We are following someone else who assures us the woods are safe, and we don't really need to examine the forest line ourselves. Why should we study the tree line? We know it's there, and we believe it to be the truth.

That is precisely why Satan wants us to look away from the forest (the Bible). If he can convince us that we know all there is to know, we will not open the true word of God, and we will be easy targets. We will not look at the forest; we will just assume it to be true without checking it out for ourselves. But concealed in the woods, a sniper may be zeroing in, and by not opening our Bibles to find the truth, we might end up in the crosshairs of the devil's rifle.

In America today, a conglomerate of people, politicians, organizations, and churches are spreading doctrines that, on the outside, appear to coincide with the true teachings of Jesus as they appear to those who don't read the actual teachings of Jesus; therefore, they don't know the true teachings of Jesus.

> For such people are false apostles, deceitful work-
> ers, masquerading as apostles of Christ. And no
> wonder, for Satan himself masquerades as an
> angel of light. It is not surprising, then, if his ser-
> vants also masquerade as servants of righteous-
> ness. Their end will be what their actions deserve.
> (2 Corinthians 11:13–15 NIV)

Those who are destined to an eternal existence away from God do not see the true teachings of Jesus. Either they reject the truth or reject the opportunity to learn the truth. By failing to take the small, yet necessary, time to read and learn from the word of God, we reject the opportunity to learn the truth and, henceforth, are presenting ourselves as open targets for the devil's lies.

When we know and understand the truth, however, the one who saved us from an eternity in hell can use us to save perhaps even our closest, most-cherished loved ones here on earth from the same dismal outcome. But if we refuse to open the curtains and allow the light to come in, then we will remain in the darkness, unable to help ourselves or anyone else. If we dwell in darkness, we cohabitate with the unsaved. We forge ahead with lies as our truth, and the truth is forever hidden.

But if we let the light in, then we can see our way clear to try to rid ourselves of sinful ways. While our flesh may still sin from time to time, we will recognize our weaknesses because our spirits will be righteous in the eyes of the Lord. We will know not to twist the truth, and our actions will be visible to others even if the they are still blind to the truth. We can then draw open the curtain for others to see.

> Rather, we have renounced secret and shameful
> ways; we do not use deception, nor do we dis-
> tort the word of God. On the contrary, by setting

forth the truth plainly we commend ourselves to everyone's conscience in the sight of God. And even if our gospel is veiled, it is veiled to those who are perishing. (2 Corinthians 4:2–3 NIV)

Whoever says "I know him," but does not do what He commands is a liar, and the truth is not in that person. (1 John 2:4 NIV)

While 1 John 2:4 is primarily addressing our requirement to love our Father in Heaven and our brothers and sisters in Christ, our true everlasting family, we are also expected to follow and obey all the Savior's commands, which include praying for and selecting righteous governmental leadership. Leaders who make decisions that contradict the teachings of the Bible are choosing to correct the Bible. These are unrighteous guides who should be removed from office at the next legal opportunity.

Prayer for the Spirit to pierce their hearts while still in office, however, could lead them to accept Christ and alter their views of Christianity and the teachings of the Bible in a most positive way. So how do we know if a candidate approves of the teachings of Jesus? Short easy answer: know the Bible yourself. Long hard answer: know the Bible yourself. How can you know the Bible? Short easy answer: read it and ask for revelation. Long hard answer: read it and ask for revelation.

One who claims to read the Bible yet still believes that an unborn baby is just a clump of lifeless tissue is either lying about reading the Bible or is consciously rejecting the word of God. One who claims to read the Bible yet still believes that marriage of two people of the same gender is okay with God (the Creator and rule maker) is either not reading the Bible or has decided that God makes mistakes.

One who claims to read and accept God's word yet maintains that all creation came from nothing either has not studied the Bible or is denying the world surrounding him or her. One who claims to be a Bible-believing Christian yet places financial gain and earthly belongings at the top of his or her agenda has either not made time to read the Bible or doesn't believe its teachings.

One who claims to have a knowledgeable relationship of the holy word of God yet continues to select candidates from a political party that openly rejects the truth of the Bible is probably flat-out lying about his or her knowledge of the word or just doesn't care about the truth. One who claims a working knowledge of the Bible yet does not understand that Jesus Christ is the God of Abraham, Isaac, and Jacob and takes offense at the Jewish people and the nation of Israel has not opened his or her mind to the truth of the Bible or is well under-read in scripture.

When one does not care about the truth as taught by Christ, then one must not care about the truth of an eternity in a place so vile that words cannot describe the horror. Hell was created for the fallen angels, the angels who chose to follow Satan in his revolt. It was never intended for us. We declared hell ours when we opted to deny the Lord God Almighty in favor of the devil. By rejecting God, we side with the spiritual and eternal revolutionaries, the enemies of God.

So how can anyone know if another person is destined for hell? Nobody can know. Only God knows for sure. Only he can read someone's heart. But outward signs can be indicators. God wants us to grow in faith through Bible study, prayer, and fellowship so we can recognize the indicators of a person who is not yet truly saved, but only deceived into a false sense of everlasting security. Only by maturing in faith can we learn to recognize the signs of an unbeliever who needs course correction.

> Do not merely listen to the word, and so deceive yourselves. Do what it says. Anyone who listens to the word but does not do what it says is like someone who looks at his face in a mirror and, after looking at himself, goes away and immediately forgets what he looks like. (James 1:22–24 NIV)

James 1:27 tells us to "keep oneself from being polluted by the world." We should all periodically examine ourselves to see that we are not believing the lies of the world. The more mature in our faith we become, the less likely Satan will succeed in manipulating us to achieve his goal of dragging souls away from our Savior. The more our faith expands, the more probable that we will learn to humble ourselves, allowing us to shatter the illusions we accept as truth.

Once born again, the newborn Christian must not stagnate in self-righteousness, considering himself or herself superior to those still dead to Jesus. Only by studying the word and searching for more truth can one increase in knowledge to the point that the Holy Spirit uses the person to reach others not yet reborn. When an individual has matured enough to understand the sinful effect pride has on one's belief system, that person becomes able to destroy the myriad of myths Satan has used to delude him or her.

To the free-thinking liberal-minded thinker of our age, restrictions of freedom are restrictions of "God-given" rights. God-given? The same individual who claims these so-called God-given rights is usually the first person to reject the "crazy Bible-toting Jesus freak" as being out of touch with today's progressive society. This free-thinking, open-minded person will accuse the Christian believer of possessing narrow-minded and bigoted worldviews.

In one way, the liberal modern thinker is correct. The true Christian believer is narrow-minded. We believe there is truth and falsehood, and there is only one truth and one falsehood. The truth is in the light of God, and the falsehood is in the darkness of Satan. The true Christian believer is also bigoted. We reject the devil without hesitation and will not accept anything he says. We try as hard as we can to restrict Satan using any intolerant method available.

While the liberal thinker of today considers himself or herself so open-minded that he or she could never be accused of intolerance, this person makes the common error of holding great intolerance to anyone who believes different than he or she, especially the "hateful narrow-minded Christian believer," and, yes, the practicing Jew. Is it just a coincidence that the born-again Christian and the practicing Jew worship the same God, albeit in simplistic terms? The difference is, the Jew is waiting for the coming Messiah, while the Christian is waiting for the second coming of the same Messiah.

This is another sign that the God of Abraham, Isaac, and Jacob is the one true God. The devil is relentlessly attacking him, attempting to convince people they don't need to read the Bible because they already know all there is to know. Satan fully understands that once a person reads the Bible and steps into the light of truth, he has lost that soul.

Considering we all are born into the sin of Adam and Eve, only the open-minded individual can actually "open" his or her mind to the possibility that the Bible's teachings are worth examining and that any truth can come from it. At one time, we also hated the "Christian fanatic" until we explored a belief system we knew nothing about. But we swallowed our pride and opened our minds to the far-flung ideas of these Christians. So I say to all the unbelievers: we too once did not believe!

The Lord won't give up trying to reach all who do not believe. If an unbeliever winds up cooking in the oven, it is his or her own fault.

> In his pride the wicked man does not seek him;
> in all his thoughts there is no room for God.
> (Psalm 10:4 NIV)

> This is how you can recognize the Spirit of god: Every spirit that acknowledges that Jesus Christ has come in the flesh is from God, but every spirit that does not acknowledge Jesus is not from God. This is the spirit of the Antichrist, which you have heard is coming and even now is already in the world. (1 John 4:2–3 NIV)

> This is how we know who the children of god are and who the children of the devil are: Anyone who does not do what is right is not God's child, nor is anyone who does not love their brother and sister. (1 John 3:10 NIV)

While we certainly love our earthly flesh-and-blood siblings, the relations John speaks of are our brothers and sisters in Christ, our everlasting family. Those who reject the holy word of God are making that decision for themselves and will have no one to blame but themselves when they end up separated from God forever.

We determine for ourselves which path to follow, the path that leads to Jesus and salvation or the path leading to eternal damnation. Those who choose damnation are those who follow their own hearts and rage against the Lord.

> A person's own folly leads to their ruin, yet their
> heart rages against the Lord. (Proverbs 19:3 NIV)

A number of organizations in America avow antibiblical standards. Many of these groups maintain the patronage of people erroneously referring to themselves as Christian. Can a true believer in the death and resurrection of Jesus who is in true repentance and whose body acts as the Lord's temple and home to the Holy Spirit of God support a group that unashamedly promotes the false teachings of the devil? Remember, there are only two kinds of teaching: (1) the truth, which comes from God and (2) all other lessons. If the teaching is not from God, it can only be from the devil. Jesus said:

> Why is my language not clear to you? Because
> you are unable to hear what I say. You belong
> to your father, the devil, and you want to carry
> out your father's desires. He was a murderer from
> the beginning, not holding to the truth, for there
> is no truth in him. When he lies, he speaks his
> native language, for he is a liar and the father of
> lies. (John 8:43–44 NIV)

The Bible clearly states that unborn babies are children of God, yet there are organizations that reap millions of dollars through the death of babies. These outfits masquerade as centers for the health and well-being of women when in fact that is a lie propagated by the devil to conceal the gruesome practice of abortion. It is Satan himself hiding the crime in the forest of women's health. The unbeliever and the uneducated believer fall for the camouflaged lie and allow for the deaths of their own and God's children.

We have all committed unspeakable crimes against the Lord. Fortunately, for our sake, Jesus is always waiting for our repentance and the opportunity to free us from any and all sin if we will only come to him seeking the truth with genuine remorse in our hearts. But we must want to be in the light of truth and repentance. Only when we are willing to leave darkness behind us will we be prepared and want to grow in faith in order to come closer to our Savior.

The book he gave us waits for us. It is the Bible that holds the knowledge of the universe, the only true teachings of the Creator of the world, and the personal Savior of each of us. Only the truly open-minded will initiate a study of the Bible. Only through at least a rudimentary examination can one have any basis on which to reject it. Only those who inaugurate a willingness to scrutinize can claim education of decision. Without an education of any subject, no one can claim to make an informed decision. An argument founded on erroneous information can only lead to the arguer falling for his or her own lies. These are the lies concocted by a closed mind to defend a truth he or she knows nothing of.

The fact that those crazy, whacked-out, Bible-toting, religious-fanatic Jesus freaks did not believe at one time is the proof they are the true open-minded people. Those are the folks who chose to actually see for themselves what this Bible stuff was all about. At first, they may have done it in secret so no one would know. But that's okay because each of us must make the decision for ourselves. Again, I say to all you "open-minded" unbelievers. We too once did not believe!

> We too all previously lived among them in our fleshly desires, carrying out the inclinations of our flesh and thoughts, and we were by nature children under wrath as the others were also. (Ephesians 2:3 HCSB)

PART 2

INTRODUCTION

An Examination of the Secret War

The shells and bullets have been flying for eons, and the conflict has been bloody. In the United States, the war between good and evil has been submerged, primarily because the United States has been a God-fearing nation for the better part of its history.

While we can argue that the United States is not and has never been a Christian nation, the majority of its believers have self-identified and continue to self-identify as Christian. Many of these self-proclaimed Christians of the past were undoubtedly deceived, false believers. It's no different today. At times, our country went through periods of religious dissention, but revival always surfaced, and the nation returned to the way of the Bible.

During much of US history, the term "born-again Christian" was simply the biblical reference to any and all true, saved souls.

> Jesus answered and said to him "Most assuredly,
> I say to you, unless one is born again, he cannot
> see the kingdom of God." (John 3:3 NKJV)
>
> Do not marvel that I said to you, "You must be
> born again." (John 3:7 NKJV)

In past times, born-again believers in the United States understood the term Jesus taught because they read their Bibles. The good book was more than just a decoration they prominently displayed at Christmas and Easter. But in times of falling away, the term has become a title. Today, "born-again Christians" are considered fanatics even by those who claim to be Christians because many among the Christian majority are, in fact, not Christian and don't even know what a Christian is.

The United States has always been considered a safe haven for the religious-minded. Citizens of the United States have always been permitted to worship as they desire. It is not a Christian nation, however, because all are allowed to practice any faith without interference from the government. It just happened to be that the dominant faith claimed has always been Christianity.

Americans are no different from any other people. In fact, America is made up of people from all over the world. Just like the rest of the world, we have differing opinions on issues such as the use of tax dollars, how to preserve open land, pollution restrictions… and faith.

How many beliefs can be true? How many gods are there since there can't be multiple creators? So which God is the real deal? There is only one faith that presents the Creator as being the only way to heaven. Other religions call attention to a single god, but only Christianity puts our salvation in the hands of God alone. Other deities make our actions the primary determining factor in our afterlife. Christianity dictates that our actions will be the result of whether we follow God. Only Christianity boasts that none of us are worthy of everlasting life with God. While none of us are worthy, he is willing to forgive us and make us worthy. Only Christianity has the undeniable evidence of accurate supernatural prophecy. Only Christianity teaches us to love our enemies as God does. The list of proofs is endless.

For the better part of the existence of the United States, this nation has accepted the Bible as the one true conduit to the teachings of God. If we have God on our side, in the end we will win. Whether an individual or a nation, when we turn to the one true God, victory is eminent; hence, the great blessings of the United States of America…until recently.

We in America have usually voted the way we prayed. We had a knowledge of the word of God, and we allowed God to influence our local and national leadership. Our country has never been flawless, but through stamina in our faith, we persevered. We have always had disagreements, but we have always been able to come together in our faith in the teachings of God. The principles of the Bible led us.

But Satan has also never been bashful about presenting us with ideas contrary to God's teachings in the Bible. Unfortunately for Satan, God warns us of his ways in the same Bible. So one who reads scripture is wearing an armored suit impervious to the daggers heaved by the devil. Sadly, all of us suffer moments of weakness and go out into the world without our armor. We leave scripture behind and allow the devil to successfully tempt us with the ways of the world, the ways of Satan.

The war between Caesar's kingdom (the secular world) and God's kingdom (the spiritual world) is waging in the United States now as it always has. While many battles have seen God the victor, Satan always remains a viable foe waiting for the next chance to attack. In the end, the devil will lose. But until then, he intends to bring as many down with him as he can.

CHAPTER 8

A Government for the People by the People Without God? The Devil Waits for Such a Chance

Do you see yourself as a Republican? A Democrat? Perhaps a libertarian? Or maybe you consider yourself the only one who's right, an open-minded independent. But wait a minute; the Democrats are the ones who are right. That independent had better think things over. No, that's not true; the Republicans represent the true Americans. Should not Socialist Communism, Fascism, and the Nazi Party be considered legitimate options as well? After all, this is a free society.

A number of Americans believe the key to happiness and peace in the world is fueled by complete and total freedom. But, to the dismay of those grossly uninformed people, a society where absolute freedom reigns is a society with no rules. Freedom without restrictions is anarchy.

The American Heritage Dictionary describes anarchy as follows:

An-ar-chy 1. Absence of any form of political authority. 2. Disorder and confusion.

So in actuality, a totally free society is a society bent on chaos, a communion of individuality with no regulation and no protection. If you have it, but I want it, it becomes mine. In a completely free nation, there is no need for police since we are free to do anything, and to make anything ours. After all, should I not be entitled to the same things somebody else has?

If someone else owns a Rolls Royce, why shouldn't I have the same? I am also entitled to live out my own in individual desires. A child molester is only expressing his natural-born needs. A rapist is only eliminating his sexual frustration, a perfectly normal thing in a rules-free land. Should I disagree with you, you need to be eliminated for my own good. It is perfectly okay for me to restrict your speech and even cause you physical pain. In the absolute free society, you should have the same right to kick my rear if we disagree.

In a nutshell, your totally free utopia is a land with no restrictions, no rules, and no regulations; a nation of disorder and confusion; and a society with no political authority to maintain order. Even the most radical freedom-first thinker must see the benefit from some form of regulation on freedom, some restrictions on what we can and cannot do.

In America, those restrictions are called laws. The penalty for breaking one of these laws depends on the particular law broken; the habituality of the law breaker; and, in some instances, a judge or a jury of citizens determining guilt and severity of the assigned punishment.

The foundations of our rules and regulations that provide for civil order can be found in the same book that so many fans of freedom and disorder disdain: the Bible. So let's take a look at just a small handful of biblical laws and compare them to the laws written in our books or our culture. Pay special attention to the change taking place in some of these examples.

1. The separation of church and state. Despite the popularity of the fraudulent claim that this declaration is somewhere in our Constitution, this statement was written by Thomas Jefferson in a personal letter determining that the state has no business sticking its nose in the doings and beliefs of the church.[12] There is no foundation to the idea that the government cannot abide by the rules of the church. On the contrary, the church is not to succumb to the secular

teaching of the state, which would be correcting God and turning the state into a false God.

While it is not illegal to worship a donkey, an elephant, or the Nazi flag, it is certainly frowned upon to turn a political party into an idol bent on nothing of any benefit but solely motivated by hatred and disagreement of any other political party. Your symbol or flag now becomes your false god.

2. The use of off-color language in a public place was once considered reason enough to condemn the perpetrator to a citation or even jail time, in the same way public nudity is sometimes viewed today. At one time, television and movies restricted the use of four-letter words in concern for public decency. One of the worst offenses was taking the Lord's name in vain, turning the name of God into a cuss word.

3. While the common use of G.D. or the flippant use of the name of Jesus Christ is mostly offensive to Christian believers, our feelings seem to mean nothing in a society where total freedom for any belief as long as it is not Christianity is the perceived way of peace. Our feelings are often overlooked, and our own hate laws are ignored when it comes to hating Christians. But God's feelings are still offended.

4. It was once common for many businesses to close on Sunday to allow employees to worship and rest. This included businesses that sold alcohol and gas for our cars. We needed to gas up the car on Saturday, or we were not driving to the country after church on Sunday.

Today, consumers chastise a business that closes on Sunday for not being concerned with the buyers holding good money in their hands. It is the company making the decision to give up those dollars, and it should have no effect on the buyer shopping elsewhere. Again, in defiance of our own hate laws, the same people who pushed for the placement of these hate crimes are the ones responsible for staging protests and boycotts of Christian-owned businesses.

5. It was once considered an unwritten law that we took care of our parents as they took care of their children. In a home where Christ was the driving force, seldom was the elderly parent considered to be in the way of the advancement of the children or grandchildren. There have always been, of course, situations where grown children have to place their older loved ones in the charge of skilled care persons. But if financial gain, not Christ, is the main priority, many claim they have no time to care for the parents who did have time to care for them three, four, or five decades earlier.

6. Murder is against the law in all federal, state, and local jurisdictions. But even murder is being challenged as god-lessness moves forward. Killing the unborn child is not considered murder unless the mother is also killed. So the people who claim so much concern for the health of the mother have no concern for the well-being of the future mother. Perhaps the solution is to kill only the infant males. President Ronald Reagan found it curious that the most diligent supporters of abortion have all been born.[13]

7. Traditionally, adultery has been an illegal activity in the United States, and, when divorce proceedings take place, the adulterer is normally held as the most responsible for the marriage break-up. According to Jesus in the Matthew 5, the only credible grounds for divorce is sexual immorality.

8. Stealing is a crime, no matter how small the theft. Just taking a pen from work could theoretically get a person fired or result in criminal charges. Auto theft or bank robbery will, of course, result in prison time.

    Could swiping a paper clip from work actually keep a soul out of heaven? Yes. As there is no need of money or any other currency in heaven, stealing a paper clip will have the same outcome to a person's eternity as stealing a million bucks. Stealing is stealing. The Savior must forgive it, just like any other biblical crime.

9. Lying under oath is punishable by jail time. In a court of law, what book does the one testifying place his or her hand

on? Other crimes with names like fraud, slander, and tax evasion are crimes of lying.

10. Jealousy and envy have traditionally been viewed as indicators of a weak character. The desire to have what the neighbor has and the need to outdo that neighbor at any cost have always been hanging around. The lust of the flesh pertains not only to sexual desire, but also the want of many things the mind may perceive to be objects providing physical pleasure or satisfaction of emotional needs. One can try to conquer jealousy by attaining more than the neighbor has, but the neighbor will always acquire something new, resulting in renewed jealousy and the need to outdo. Socialism is a brand of governing whose root cause is greed and envy. All of us must have what the few at the top have, and everyone is then equal.

When people push for Socialism, they are generally expressing a deeply pent-up feeling of jealousy and are most likely not willing to accept the fact that those who have more than they have, for the most part, earned their prosperity through much effort. Sometimes, the effort was questionable to the point of criminality, but not always. Just because someone has more than I do does not mean they earned it illegally. Even the successful crooks had to work for it.

This is why envy and jealousy have been frowned upon by tradition. They are characteristics of a person not willing to work for benefit. Does "lazy" ring a bell? For the person who works and earns something through his or her own sweat, be it physical or mental sweat, a sense of achievement occurs that can greatly alleviate the need to envy.

Socialism is a theory that allows for the confiscation of private holdings of the few for the betterment of the many. The problem with this system of government is when the belongings of the few have been exhausted, then the holdings of the few at the top of the many must be seized to accommodate the entitlement of the rest of the many. In a short time, the many are the few, and the few are the many. When those who had the very least now have all that is left, they are required to surrender their meager belongings to the only

165

one left who can try to restore order to a society now rampant with starvation and poverty. The dictator takes control of all.

To the longing Socialist, remember, you too have more than somebody else. If you are prepared to take a totally free education, accept completely free health care, latch on to a free home, you must also be prepared to give all that you have to the person below you. Should you choose the field of medicine with your free education, will you be willing to spend your career treating others for free so they too can have free health care?

So as you can see, Socialism is the ultimate free society. Everyone has nothing, and the ruler makes all the laws. And, by the way, God is a challenger to the earthly Socialist dictator, so our Bibles will be outlawed and our heads will roll. Literally!

The Socialist theory is nothing new. It has led to the fall of many nations. The first Socialist to run for president of the United States of America was Simon Wing of Massachusetts in 1892. Mr. Wing garnered 21,164 votes from a total 12,053,259 ballots cast. That means he scooped up 0.0017558 percent of the vote, a little less than $2/10^{th}$ of one percent. A Socialist has been on the presidential ballot at dozen times since 1892.

While a Socialist party has been hanging around America for more than one hundred years, it usually fails to generate enough support to place a candidate on the presidential ballot and attempts to sneak into power from the bottom-up. Until recently, the people of the United States had enough biblical fortitude to resist this back-door effort of the godless Socialist party to eradicate biblical values.

It is the devil's patience that is responsible for the slow erosion of Christian values in our country. Satan sits back and quietly introduces ideas that seem biblical while all the time he is subtly convincing a once well-read Christian nation to put Bible study aside and accept the seemingly more appetizing lies from the dark side as the real truth, which, of course, is the "new truth." The well-informed Christian believer knows and understands this new truth is just the same old lie from that old liar himself.

The devil uses the joys of a totally free Socialist regime as subterfuge to eradicate the words of Jesus. By putting the Bible aside, we can attain this great freedom. The Bible has too many rules to live by and is not cohesive with a Socialist governing party.

Will a Socialist regime in the United States provide free health care, education, and housing? Yes. Until the money is all gone. With no real need to work, there will be no tax base, and the free goodies will disappear. With nobody willing to work for free, to allow for the free entitlements, there will be no staff at the doctors' offices and no food on the grocery store shelves. We will be entirely on our own.

But we won't be on our own for long. There will always be a willing dictator to promise relief. While there has never been a communist who ran a successful campaign for president of the United States, the Communist Party does exist. So does the Nazi party, the KKK, and a wide assortment of other godless hate organizations representing every race, creed, gender, etc. In reality, these groups do not represent white people, black people, women, men, or anyone else. They represent Satan, the hater of Jesus and the leader of all that is evil.

The ruse Satan uses to persecute a particular group of people will cause a particular class to preach hate against another class under the guise of self-persecution. Even though persecution may have actually occurred, the solution is not reverse persecution. The answer is found in God's teachings, the teachings of Jesus while he was here on earth.

The devil, however, will continue his relentless battle of deception until he finds success. He will lean on whatever lie he needs in order to eliminate God from human society. The line separating Communism from Socialism is a thin one, but they have two things in common:

1. All people will be equal.
2. There is no room for division caused by the existence of God.

Does number 1 sound pretty fair? Sure it does. We will all be equally under the catastrophic administration of a single, and highly probable, vicious dictator. Socialism is a bridge to Communism. A Communist dictatorship is a disaster to all, and the first to suffer will be the believer. We must never presume anything good can come about apart from God.

CHAPTER 9

The Rules of Battle Are in Place Each of Us Must Select a Side

Now that we have briefly examined a bit of the outer fringe of politics and Socialism, let's have a look at the more mainstream political parties vying for control of the United States and see how they stand up to the test of political correctness vs. biblical correctness.

Political correctness is usually associated with fairness for all at the expense of any cohesive family values. In a truly politically correct society, family values must generally be put aside because they are quite often in harmony with biblical values, which include the definition of marriage is between one man and one woman, the life of the unborn is as sacred as the life of the already born, God made only man and woman in his image, there is only one true God, and he created the heavens and the earth. There is normally little concern for the desires and rights of those who take to the biblical view of an issue because anything that obstructs someone else's desires is in the way of political correctness.

Right off the bat, the hypocrisy of political correctness should be evident to all. In the name of fairness to all, there is only one view. Anyone who disagrees with the correct view must be eliminated. So where does fairness for all fit in with this since the only correct view is the one viewed by the correct? This is not fair at all. It is contemplated treachery by the devil to mask his scheme to rid the world of faith in Christ.

To be truly fair, Christianity is not all inclusive. Biblical values are not everyone's choice, and the Bible-believing Christian makes no excuses about it. A person either accepts the truth of God or does not. The true Christian makes no pretense of being politically correct. We believe that God makes the rules, Jesus was sent to save us, and it is up to us to decide whether to choose to repent and accept the gift of grace. Since we believe and understand the consequences of rejecting Jesus, we would be selfish indeed not to warn others of the reality of hell.

Yet, by sincerely wanting to see others saved from the horror of an eternity in hell, nonbelievers accuse us of being hateful and divisive in society. We must be eliminated, therefore, for the fairness of all. Even though we realize we cannot force others to accept Christ, it is a key part of our faith to tell others about Jesus and to make sure to sound the alarm to the reality of hell. If we believe in the real existence of heaven and hell, it only seems a normal result of this faith would be to warn others of this truth out of concern for their eternal welfare. Where is the hatred in this?

It makes no difference if the Christian is right or wrong about an afterlife and the existence of heaven and hell. Assuming the Christian believes in such an afterlife (and any true Bible-believing Christian will), nonbelievers can only accuse us of concern for the welfare of others when we tell them of our belief. It makes no difference if we are silly and gullible to believe in such a thing. We are only trying to help others. Unfortunately, we are often the recipients of coarse language and vile threats.

In the physical world, we can be politically correct as long as we leave that Christian baggage behind. The world sees those Christian values and ideas as roadblocks on the highway to fairness for all, including the choice of the pregnant woman. In fact, by the world's standards, the biblically correct have no concern for the welfare of the pregnant mother. So biblical correctness is seen as narrow-minded and hateful.

Unfortunately for nonbelievers, the opposite of life is death, not choice. In fact, God says there is no choice. We are not to kill each other! And in reality, the opposite of biblical correctness is Satanic correctness, not political correctness. It cannot be said enough: to reject the Bible is to reject Jesus. To reject Jesus is to accept Satan.

While the politically correct mask their hate for Christian values with the lie of fairness for all, the biblically correct make no effort to hide their disdain of the devil and his wicked values. So, yes, we embrace our narrow-minded vision. We make every attempt to destroy our pride and let God lead us. We genuinely try to submit and follow our Savior. We read the Bible, and we accept its teachings. We are known as the evangelical voting group.

In the first two decades of the twenty-first century, there has been one political party courting the evangelicals while the other party has largely conducted a campaign against the belief system of the evangelical voting block. This particular party has chosen to build an entire agenda dedicated to rallying any voter who is willing to claim that evangelical believers in Christ are hate mongers bent on arresting all who disagree with their Christian agenda. It is likely that these people are confusing the love of Jesus with Sharia law of radical Islam.

Interestingly enough, the people who don't accept the teachings of Jesus are the ones instigating the arrest of the Jesus followers, referred to as Christian evangelicals. This happens to be exactly what is happening throughout the world in any nation founded on Islam. While these politically correct groups usually claim no religious faith, they tend to side with the extreme measures of Sharia law when it comes to dealing with the evangelicals. This leads to a conclusion that the politically correct side is joined with Islam in its rejection of the word of God. So, again, it must be stated that the enemy of biblical correctness is Satanic correctness, masquerading as political correctness.

As a true believer in the word God, a self-proclaiming Christian should understand that any enemy of Jesus is an ally of Satan. Jesus warned us of persecution by unbelievers in the gospel of Mark when he stated:

> You must be on your guard. You will be handed over to the local councils and flogged in the synagogues. On account of me you will stand before governors and kings as witnesses to them. (Mark 13:9 NIV)

> Whenever you are arrested and brought to trial,
> do not worry about what to say. Just say whatever
> is given you at the time, for it is not you speak-
> ing, but the Holy Spirit. (Mark 13:11 NIV)

These arrests are occurring in the United States. Just ask Kim Davis of Kentucky. In 2014, she was elected as clerk of Rowan County. Several months after her election, on June 26, 2015, a US Supreme Court decision required by a 5-4 vote that the individual states could no longer have a say on the marriage issue.[14] All Kentucky clerks were now to issue marriage licenses to gay couples. The fact that people such as Kim Davis openly worshiped the God of the Bible and chose to follow the teachings of God regarding marriage was never considered. Her rights as a Christian were trampled in favor of the perceived rights of the godly defiant.

While Kim Davis never scorned the gay community, she understood the teachings of the Bible and was able to fathom the fact that we are all sinners. She comprehends that this does not mean we have the right to openly break the rules of our faith. In an effort to be fair to all without breaking the law of Jesus, she chose not to issue marriage licenses to gay couples. These people were under no obligation to receive their licenses from Davis and were perfectly capable of getting them elsewhere. A Kentucky marriage license is a Kentucky marriage license, no matter who grants it.

Much of the gay community decided, however, that the religious rights of others were of no value and needed to be eliminated with no exception. Kim Davis was arrested and jailed on contempt of court charges to the celebratory cheers of the godless left and the majority of the claimed homosexual population.

While the gay couples involved in the case could have gotten married elsewhere, they chose to practically demand Davis' imprisonment. The insistence that Davis, and no one else, issued their license was either an indication of extreme childishness or the sign of hatred to any and all who disagree with them.

The Supreme Court of the United States has elected to spit in the face of religious freedom by choosing to stand with that portion of a group of people who openly despise Christians and the God they worship. The government of the United States of America has openly granted this Christian phobia authentic recognition by actually allowing regulations that prohibit believers of the teachings of Jesus to manifest their faith through action. So this nation has now begun imprisoning people of faith.

Christian civilians are being attacked regularly. Just ask Jack Phillips of Masterpiece Cake shop Ltd. in Colorado. There is no evidence of the artistic bakery refusing to serve anyone, including homosexual patrons, until a gay couple asked this small Christian-owned business to bake a creation in celebration of something that violated the religious belief of the shop owner.

The homosexual couple could have respected the faith of the bakeshop management and gone to any one of a million other places to get the cake for their event, but, in an act of hostility and narrow-minded hatred for the Christian faith, the gay couple chose to persecute the Christian-owned business. Mr. Phillips reflecting his faith in his business decisions is nothing new. He regularly refuses to design cakes for Halloween, divorce, bachelor parties, and other events that conflict with his faith.[15]

In a show of vile hatred for Christ, the Colorado Civil Rights Commission attempted to humiliate Phillips by requiring him to file quarterly "compliance" reports detailing the reasons he might have for declining to make a cake.[16] The commission also ordered him to teach his employees that he was wrong for not denying his faith. In other words, his own state required him to indoctrinate his employees, who are mostly family, to disrespect their own Christian beliefs. So, folks, if you are a believer of Christ, you are not welcome in Colorado.

The title "Colorado Civil Rights Commission" needs to be amended so all will understand what they truly believe. A more accurate title might be "Colorado Civil Rights Commission (Christian civil rights not included)." Kim Davis and Jack Phillips are only two examples of Christian phobia. A few cases have become dozens, and dozens have become hundreds. The growth of anti-Christian and anti-Semitic rhetoric has grown past the state of alarm and has reached the outskirts of full-blown persecution. In many parts of the world, this persecution is at full ancient-Rome standards. Radical Islam is beheading, burning alive, drowning, and crucifying Christian men, women, children, and, most horrendous of all, babies of Christian families.

Do you identify as Christian and think it can't happen in America? Think again. Twenty years ago, the United States government was not shutting down Christian businesses, companies were not firing Christians for sharing their beliefs or for carrying a Bible, and the police were not arresting Christians. You who identify as Christian, have you opened your Bible in the last year, or five, or twenty years? If not, there is a good chance you support the persecution without even knowing it.

The division in America in the early 2000s is supernatural. To those who live sequestered by the dark lies of Satan, the divide is the result of religious fanaticism and purely manufactured by mankind. But the true believer should smell a rat. This kind of division is more than the division we might see among baseball fans. The division between the American League and the National League may create an argument that could get heated, but the division between political beliefs is tearing families apart. The kind of division our nation is experiencing in the early twenty-first century is unrest of biblical proportions. Jesus said:

> Brother will betray brother to death, and a father his child. Children will rebel against their parents and have them put to death. Everyone will hate you because of me, but the one who stands firm to the end will be saved. (Mark 13:12–13 NIV)

Most saved believers can recognize spiritual warfare. The spiritual war has been ongoing since Satan rebelled, but in the United States, it seems to have flared dramatically beginning in the 1960s with the elimination of prayer in schools, the American government's official acceptance of abortion, and the sexual revolution.

In the early 2000s, the war seems about to go nuclear. The gulf between the left and the right has grown to a distance intimidating even to the likes of Evel Knievel. It is the width of that gulf that stands out as evidence of true spiritual warfare. This is not a mere difference of opinion; it is a great chasm. It is the same chasm that separated the rich man from Lazarus the beggar, the very chasm that is the impenetrable barrier dividing heaven from hell. It is the struggle between good and evil, the war between God and Satan.

But how did the United States reach such a repugnant state of division? Why are the American people so hateful of the other side that we can't bring ourselves to even consider the opinion of someone who identifies as a member of the other political party? The answer is more obvious than you might think.

The Democratic Party is not the Democratic Party of old, and the Republican Party is not the Republican Party of days past. In fact, the two parties exist in name only. The time when a Republican and a Democrat could disagree on secular issues but come together on social issues has passed away. Today, most Ds and Rs can't even agree to defend our nation in times of external assault.

Could we all celebrate the downfall of Saddam Hussein? Only half the nation found joy in the capture of the sadistic dictator. Could we all jump for joy at the demise of bin Laden? It seems not all rejoiced at the elimination of this representative of evil.

The two parties do not exist anymore. But they have not gone the way of the Federalists, Whigs, Freesoilists, Greenbacks, Prohibitionists, and States Rights parties. The Democrats and the Republicans did not vanish in the same way that the Constitutional Unionists, Farmer Laborers, and Liberty parties disappeared. Even the old "Democratic-Republican" party died a more dignified death.

The Democratic-Republican Party won the presidency seven times between 1800 and 1824, but they are a distant memory today, only referred to in American history books and some other books and periodicals of interest to political history buffs. The mainstream education system in America today seems to regard early American history with disdain because many of our founding fathers intermingled biblical instruction with secular teaching.

It is folly to claim the spread between the left and the right is growing primarily due to the escalating extremism by one side more than the other. Both sides are guilty of heightened extremism, and this is the specific indication of a momentous battle being engaged by two parties that are polar opposites of one another.

When God and Satan do battle there is no gray area. There can be no compromise. The devil slipped into the American political system through subterfuge, which is his favorite tactic. He accomplished great victories in the United States beginning in the middle of the twentieth century when he convinced an entire nation that the teachings of God had no place being involved with the teachings of man. He seduced a country founded on biblical values and convinced the leaders of that country that biblical values stood in the way of progress.

The devil managed to prompt a God-fearing people to believe it is a woman's right to choose the life or death of her own child. Satan induced a great nation to indulge in all sorts of sexual behavior at the expense of monogamous marriage between one man and one woman. These were only the early stages of Satan's attacks on America. Since then, he has succeeded at eliminating an entire political party that has fallen under his spell, rejecting the light of Christ at any given chance. While this political party lives on in name, it bears no resemblance to the party it once was.

Today, the leadership of this party has built a cornerstone agenda based upon the complete annihilation of the Christian faith, going so far as to preach godless socialism as the next stage of evolution in the forward progress of our nation and the world. Under the format of this progress is the elimination of any and all public mention of Christianity and Judaism. Hence, the rising interest in godless socialism.

Socialism never has and never will lead to freedom of the people. Socialism always has and always will lead to Satan's enslavement of the people, and he will control the dictator of those enslaved people. The chains binding the slaves will be the sin of rejecting Jesus. Living in the dark world of Satan, the people in bondage will find freedom only by allowing the Savior to "save" them. When they turn to the light of true freedom, the freedom Jesus provides, they will escape the clutch of the devil.

Since the devil has gained control of one party through misrepresenting the teachings of Jesus, the people of America, both D and R, who are in the word of Christ have fled. But where could they go? It seems the other party has been masquerading as the party that chooses God. In reality, many members of this other party were not strong enough in the word to have the backbone to stand up to the heat of popular, misinformed opinion. It turns out they were demons wearing Christian costumes.

The believers finally woke up and asked for a leader who would give them a chance to be free to spread the word as Jesus instructed. Our prayer seemed answered in the election of 2016. A man of such coarseness had not taken the oval office since Harry Truman. This man seemed an easy target for the satanically correct. The devil could have a field day with his past. But the true believer understood his past was no different than anybody else's past. We all have more sin than necessary to sink us forever.

This president strikes such anger in his enemies because he was once one of them. He believed in the politically correct creed. But something turned him. God knocked on his door, and he did more than just peek through the window to see who was there. He opened the door. He flung open his mind and stepped into the light of truth.

Like all who become born-again, born spiritually into the family of Christ, he needed to grow. He would remain an infant in his faith unless he would study the word and pray for guidance. While this new leader would exhibit signs of immaturity in his faith, he still appeared to be born-again and an answer to millions of prayers. He had the strength to withstand a relentless assault from all sides. While his gruffness seemed to mimic the unsaved, his will to stand in defense of Christian values as taught in the Bible showed evidence of a man of greater faith maturity than many expected.

The winner of the 2016 presidential election seems even more of an answer to prayers than previously supposed. His tough, almost streetwise manner, seems just what the doctor ordered to weather the flailings of the devil. When God makes a plan, it's gonna work as long as we don't get in the way or fail to follow his instructions. Without trying to predict the future, it seems that God has planned a revival in the United States, or he has at least put the pieces together for us to follow through. The man is in place to follow the ice breaker that is Trump.

Mike Pence appears to be a believer of great stature as well; he's just a little less pragmatic and a bit more diplomatic than Trump. Pence, however, does not possess the secular fortitude of the ice breaker. Once the path to national repentance has been opened, it is likely that God will use Pence to guide us as a nation back to Jesus, or at least assure us the freedom to spread the word of God.

If we should fail to live up to our end of the bargain by once again falling into a state of spiritual apathy, God will once again leave us to our own will, and this time the nation will certainly fall under the full control of evil.

God answered our prayers in 2016, but if once again we put our heads in the sand like cowards, we will have wasted a wonderful opportunity to turn the nation around. It is absolutely essential, therefore, that all of us use this God-given opportunity to spread the word of Jesus. If you don't go to church, start going. Read your Bible so you understand the true teachings of Jesus, and if your church does not teach this, you need to act in one of two ways:

1. Confront the church leadership with the truth of Jesus. You absolutely have nothing to fear when doing this. If you read it in the Bible and understand it, you are representing God, which means the big man upstairs has got your back. In other words, just because someone went to seminary or is an elder or a deacon in the church does not mean they are invincible to the temptations of the stinker from down under. Some pastors are more interested in filling seats than saving souls.

2. Leave and find a biblically correct church. Any pastor who feels the need to be politically correct is doing so at the expense of biblically correct doctrine. It is more important to see one person genuinely saved by biblical doctrine than

a thousand pretend to be saved through politically correct (false) doctrine.

> Preach the word; be prepared in season and out of season; correct, rebuke and encourage-with great patience and careful instruction. For the time will come when people will not put up with sound doctrine. Instead, to suit their own desires, they will gather around them a great number of teachers to say what their itching ears want to hear. They will turn their ears away from the truth and turn aside to myths. But you, keep your head in all situations, endure hardship, do the work of an evangelist, discharge all the duties of your ministry. (2 Timothy 4:2–5 NIV)

You can't rebuke the devil unless you have the knowledge to do so. With this being understood, simple knowledge without spiritual growth means nothing. When you study the Bible with the intent of using your newfound knowledge to grow in your personal relationship with Jesus and to help others find the glory of the Savior, you will mature in faith and be of enhanced use for the Holy Spirit to speak through you. We allowed the devil to take control of the leadership of the once-faithful liberal party. The Democratic Party in America was once made up of biblically correct believers, but over the last sixty years, the god of misinformation penetrated this party and slowly converted it to a group that thrives on attacking the evangelical right.

The true believers in America have no one to blame but themselves. Since the 1960s, we have been resting in idle while the devil has been acting. We have done nothing but wait for God to intervene. Satan has lied to the ensuing generations, leading them to faith in man's ability to control his own destiny without the interference of the great Creator and rule-maker. Meanwhile, the faithful in Christ have buried our heads in the sand and allowed the nation to redefine the terms "born again" and "evangelist" as "religious fanatic" and "hate monger." We have nearly lost the skill and the will to tell others about Christ.

But where there is a will, there is a way. The will comes from the Holy Spirit, and the way is found in the word of God. We may have finally woken up. In the nick of time, we have begun to pray and ask for guidance en masse. While Satan has almost completely conquered the left, the right is reorganizing. The old guard of the Republican Party is being thrown in the trash to make room for the new conservatism; the true conservatism; the red, white, and blue conservatism. The conservatism and yes, the liberalism of old, is fighting back, and we have called on our Savior for help. But we must keep up the good fight. We are the hands and feet of God, and we are expected to act in our faith, no matter the circumstance.

Forget the lies of the devil. Satan readily uses earthly political parties of all persuasions. Only the teachings of God can lead us down the straight and narrow path. So take your political support to the true kingdom, the kingdom the Pharisees and Romans did not understand. If you do not understand where the kingdom of God is, or if you think that man is within his rights to correct the teachings in the Bible, you better alter your position before it is too late. Do not let the devil use your pride to condemn you forever.

Align with the party of righteousness, the party of the kingdom that is not of this earth. Remember that when you vote in favor of unbiblical truths, you cast a ballot in favor of pro-satanic truths. We must remain on the path without veering one way or the other, for at the end of the route is eternal reward.

> However, I consider my life worth nothing to me, my only aim is to finish the race and complete the task the Lord Jesus has given me—the task of testifying to the good news of God's grace. (Acts 20:24 NIV)

> I have fought the good fight, I have finished the race, I have kept the faith. Now there is in store for me the crown of righteousness, which the

Lord, the righteous judge, will award to me on
that day—and not only to me, but also to all who
have longed for his appearing. (2 Timothy 4:7–8
NIV)

Are you a true saved believer, or are you allowing yourself to be
entwined in lies and hatred bases on some silly human notion of right
and wrong? If you hate someone because of that individual's sin, you
must also hate yourself, as you are just as guilty. We must put blinders
on in order to stay focused on the road in front. God requires us to
forgive if he is to forgive us. Satan has peppered with landmines the
road to freedom from sin. The Holy Spirit is our mine detector, and
we cannot afford to ignore the warning signals the Spirit emits to us.

When a person refers to biblical principles and teachings, we
need to have the courage to listen because the enemy will likely have
maligned that person, and we need to stand with that persecuted
believer. Sometimes, that individual will be the leader of a nation
God has put in place as an answer to the prayers of the righteous.
That official will be besieged by the devil who is frantically trying to
unseat the person from power. If that leader has the strength of faith
and the power of salvation, however, he or she will not fade.

Anytime hate inspires attacks on any individual, you can be sure
the devil is orchestrating the onslaught, especially when the attacks
are of a personal nature. Even the righteous experience anger; it is
usually directed at the sin of a nature that directly assaults the teachings of Jesus. While we are all fallen and sometimes succumb to the
taunts of the evil one, the saved generally accept the guilt and the
shame associated with repentance. In other words, when the saved
sin, we usually feel bad, and, if our faith is mature enough, we even
try to make amends.

Among the unsaved, however, the noxious fumes of Satan
remain ever present and increase in nature. In the early twenty-first
century, the abominable hatred toward evangelically supported
political candidates seems proof of a spiritual assault on all things
Christian.

To all who actively support an organization that abounds with anger toward the evangelicals (those who read and try to absorb the word of God), you must ask yourself, "Do I really believe in the scriptures?" It is certain that there are deceived evangelicals out there. It is also certain that the percentage of folks who read the Bible with open hearts and identify as born-again Christians are far less likely to be fooled and led down the path to everlasting doom.

So if you want to make sure you are on the road to Jesus and want to place leaders with sound biblical values in public office, you absolutely need to open your Bible and ask the Holy Spirit to pierce your heart with the knowledge, understanding, and acceptance of the truth of Jesus Christ your Savior.

If you repent from your heart, are willing to forgive those who trespass against you (don't worry; the Holy Spirit will help; remember, Jesus frees us), and believe that Jesus died to pay your sin debt and rose on the third day to defeat death forever, you will be saved. You will never die. You will live forever in the presence of the Lord.

> Therefore, there is now no condemnation for those who are in Christ Jesus, because through Christ Jesus the law of the Spirit who gives you life has set you free from the law of sin and death. (Romans 8:1–2 NIV)

CHAPTER 10

The Demise of the Two-Party System
The Rise of the Single Kingdom

America is locked in a spiritual war!

Good and evil are fighting to gain jurisdiction over a single kingdom.

The United States's political system is a two-party system. The option is always present for a third party, and there have been many instances when a third party arose to challenge the norm, but that party seldom got further than a foot in the door and wound up backing into oblivion, missing a foot.

We have not always had only the Democrats and Republicans to choose from. From 1792 until 1816, we had to choose either a Federalist or a Democratic Republican.

The first Democrat to challenge for the presidency was Andrew Jackson in 1828. He won the office, and the Democratic Party was off and running. There has not been an election for the nation's top job without a Democrat in the race since.

Beginning in 1836, the chief competitor to the Dems were the Whigs. The nation's first economic depression occurred in 1837, which was the basis for the Whigs's march to victory in 1840. The Whigs and Democrats would duke it out for the ensuing forty years, facing occasional challenges from short-lived parties such as the Liberty Party, the Free Soil Party, and the Constitutional Unionist Party. In 1856, Millard Fillmore of New York was the candidate of the American (the Know-Nothing party).

Fillmore garnered more than 20 percent of the vote for a third-place finish, but the big story was the runner-up. While suffering defeat to Democrat, James Buchanan, John C. Fremont of California scooped up more than a third of the vote total and 114 electoral votes while representing the upstart Republican Party.

While many in public office were against slavery, they usually felt it better for the nation to keep the peace and not create waves. Abolition was not a new topic, but it was now becoming a hot topic. John C. Fremont and the new Republican Party seemed more interested in taking the subject of slavery seriously, which was a threat to the southern slave-holding states, the very states the Democratic Party counted on for political success.

James Buchanan was a Pennsylvanian with little reason to support slavery, but he was content to cave into the pressures of the proslavery contingent to prevent violence, much the same as many of his predecessors. Putting end to slavery in the United States would require courage, spiritual maturity, and strength.

The slave states went political to defend the institution of slavery. They claimed it was the right of individual states to determine slavery's legality. The slave states found it indispensable that federal leadership be weak on the subject. The greatest fear of the slave owner was that a governmental leader with biblical fortitude would arise from the school of slavery abolition. The man they feared most was Abraham Lincoln of this upstart Republican Party.

When Lincoln unsuccessfully ran for the Senate seat from Illinois in 1858, he proclaimed slavery a moral issue and became a national figure of note. While his opponent, the incumbent Stephen Douglas, refused to make known his position on the issue, Mr. Lincoln was most open on his view of slavery. While he claimed he was more concerned with stabilizing the Union than ending slavery, Lincoln proclaimed that under his administration, slavery would not be permitted to spread. He desired that no new state would be a slave-holding state.

Lincoln did not approve of slavery but felt it crucial to the survival of the union to not interfere with slavery where it already existed. Mr. Lincoln felt confident that slavery in the United States would wither and die on its own. The remaining civilized world had abolished slavery decades earlier, and Lincoln understood that many of these countries would soon stop trading with slave-owning establishments. He also likely assumed that many abolitionist northern businesses would cease doing business with slave holders.

Lincoln plainly stated he had no intention of banning slavery where it already existed, but he preferred it not be allowed to spread. He felt by preserving the Union, freedom would permit the self-destruction of slavery.

Today, some blather about Lincoln secretly supporting slavery. Nonsense! In a letter dated April 6, 1859, and addressed to "Henry L. Pierce and others," Lincoln wrote: "This is a world of compensation; and he who would be no slave must consent to have no slave. Those who deny freedom to others deserve it not for themselves, and, under a just God, cannot long retain it." Lincoln's antislavery sentiment is readily available to any researcher possessing the puniest resolve.

The idea of restricting the spread of slavery was pretty bold at the time, and the proslavery people feared a Lincoln presidency would attempt to outlaw slavery everywhere. As Lincoln rarely hesitated to voice his negative opinion of slavery, the slaveholders did have a basis for their concern. When Mr. Lincoln became President Lincoln, his opposition exploded with anger and panic. They saw the end coming. The chains would be broken, and bondage would disappear. Their way of life would soon be gone.

As peculiar as it seems, a whole group of people who claimed Christianity found it within themselves to support the enslavement of others. There was quite a bit of ignorance at the time, probably perpetrated by the media of the day. Having never seen or spoken to an African, many only believed what they read. Greed was their motivation, and pride did not allow them to accept a group of people they once felt superior over were actually their equals.

In their hatred of a man who regularly quoted scripture, and, by all outward signs was a true born-again Christian, the slave-holding talking heads seceded from the union, fired on Fort Sumter, and began a war that cost the lives of six hundred thousand Americans.

In the end, righteousness prevailed, but the man God had apparently used to answer the prayers of the Christian abolitionists would be assassinated. Abraham Lincoln was a national leader of special strength. He may not have been Moses, but he certainly had the biblical understanding and fortitude to withstand the full onslaught of the enemy.

Five days after the end of the war that preserved the union and freed millions of slaves, Satan used his personal troops to murder the man God used to free a people. And look what is being said about Lincoln by some on the contemporary left. Today, some on the contemporary far-left now vilify Abe Lincoln as a white supremacist. This is a display of the fact that the same hatred of the 1860s is still around. This is not surprising, as it is being propagated by the same devil.

Satan's hate never dies, and he distorts truth to meet his needs. Just consider the book written in 2000 by Lerone Bennett, *Abraham Lincoln's White Dream.*[17] The book was widely criticized for leaving out facts and distorting the truth, including truth by the widely known and respected Civil War historian James McPherson.[18,19]

Since the end of the war between the states, the Democratic and the Republican parties have been the two big boys in the political arena. They have survived much turmoil and many threats from third parties. The Republicans practically owned the winner's circle from the Civil War almost to the turn of the twentieth century. The only serious challengers to the Republicans and the Democrats during this stretch were the Greenbacks and the Prohibitionists. The Prohibition Party hung around through the start of World War II, but they were not alone in getting the eighteenth amendment pushed through. Progressives from all corners were responsible for the ultimate ratification of that amendment.

By the time Prohibition had become law on January 29, 1919, thirty-three states had already legislated regulations on alcohol. Yes, it was the progressives who chose to alter society for the better by banning alcohol. At the time, a progressive was a person of faith, interested in directing the nation down the path of righteousness.

For some time, the Lutherans had been leading the charge to curtail the use of booze, but they felt the devil was using alcohol to lead people away from God. Many politicians of that era agreed, as many were members of the faith. So Prohibition was actually a response from God to the prayers of many believers.

I am not condoning the use of alcohol, nor am I claiming it is the source of all evil. There is nothing biblically wrong with tasting and enjoying a good stout or ale. It is the abuse of alcohol from which God directs us.

> Listen, my son, and be wise, and set your heart on the right path: Do not join n those who drink too much wine or gorge themselves on meat, for drunkards and gluttons become poor, and drowsiness clothes them in rags. (Proverbs 23:19–21 NIV)

> The night is nearly over; the day is almost here. So let us put aside the deeds of darkness and put on the armor of light. Let us behave decently, as in the daytime, not in carousing and drunkenness, not in sexual immorality and debauchery, not in dissension and jealousy. Rather, clothe yourselves with the Lord Jesus Christ, and do not think about how to gratify the desires of the flesh. (Romans 13:12–14 NIV)

> For you have spent enough time in the past doing what pagans choose to do—living in debauchery, lust, drunkenness, orgies, carousing and detestable idolatry. They are surprised that you do not join them in their reckless, wild living, and they heap abuse on you. But they will have to give account to him who is ready to choose the living and the dead. (1 Peter 4:3–5 NIV)

Other scriptures that talk about the alcohol issue are 1 Corinthians 5:11 and 6:10, Galatians 5:21, Ephesians 5:21, and 1 Timothy 3:3.

Someone who claims Christianity as his or her own should not be tempting another to join him or her in violating the teachings of the Bible. We who are true believers will not be partaking in overindulgence and certainly not egging on others to do so.

At this point in the book, it is my prayer that the reader who may not be a regular student of the word of God will be inspired to start examining it. All issues in our lives are covered in God's word to us. I mean everything. The Big Guy did not forget anything. Sometimes he expects us to search a little deeper, and if we do, we will uncover our answers.

The Salvation Army and other organizations who spearheaded the temperance movement from the 1900s to 1933 may have been looked at as teetotalling fanatics, but the basis of their concern was biblically inspired and a result of the biblical prophecy of Proverbs 23:21. Alcohol was leading to a social breakdown and an increase of violence, including domestic violence.

There were many other temperance movements in the United States and elsewhere long before the appearance of the street-corner crooners of the Salvation Army. In every case, the antialcohol rage grew out of the necessity to combat unemployment and increased violence. As one early instance, temperance movements sprouted up in what was known as the "Gin Craze" in pre–1820 Great Britain.

While some supporters of the temperance movement can be threatening and drive people away from God's teaching on the subject, that does not negate the benefit of abstaining as taught in the Bible.

In 1919, the United States went dry, and that crafty old Satan, who never tires of attacking, launched a new offensive. The temptation to get loaded had not been eliminated, but the means to accomplish the task had been removed, or so it was thought. The citizenry still craved the illegal juice, and there were plenty of hard hearts who saw the opportunity to provide and make a quick buck, lots and lots of quick bucks.

The good providers from the Al Capone school of business began producing hooch in vast quantities. The stuff they turned out rotted the consumers' guts and filled the producers' pockets. So Satan was still tempting people with drink, and he presented a whole new temptation to those willing to risk the chance of incarceration. Bootlegging was so profitable that it launched a whole wave of violence. In order to garner more territory, the booze makers were not shy about threatening, beating, maiming, and even killing.

The greed became so enthralling that an entire industry grew from it. The illegal liquor business sprouted all sorts of tentacles. The felonious heads of boozedom would venture into gambling, prostitution, kidnapping, bank robbery, money laundering, blackmail, drug distribution, and anything else they could think of. This branching out needed organization. The most aggressive criminal minds rose to the top through deception and murder. In most cases, they went down the same way, in a hail of bullets. But that's the game of organized crime.

Murder, theft, sexual immorality, deception. Obviously, the game rules were created by that special gamesman from down under. The game could not thrive without a market. That market is you and me. But we don't have to fall for the advertising. While the lust of life is being thrust in our direction every time we turn around, those of us who have the Holy Spirit residing within have the tool and the power to break away from the temptation and bondage of sin. The only place to find said Spirit is in the grace of God. Going to church once in a while without bearing the grace of God as a born-anew Christian is not going to protect us from the devil, any more than putting an ice cube in the shade on an eighty-degree day will prevent it from melting.

In the 1920s, Americans flocked to the nearest den of vice. Whatever the temptation was, Americans were jumping on it. The roar in the roaring 20s was coming from the throat of Satan. The stock market crash in 1929, which triggered the Great Depression of 1930s, may or may not have been God's response to a nation and world that had chosen to reject him in favor of the pleasures of the flesh. While God does not frown on us enjoying ourselves through wholesome and innocent activities, the activities America enjoyed in the 1920s were not something anyone would take home to Mom.

Following World War I, the United States was soaring to leadership of the world, so it may not have been a coincidence that our financial crash spread worldwide. The rise of fascism in Europe came out of the results of World War I and the Depression. People were searching for a way out of misery and were looking in all the wrong places. When we inquire from the wrong source, we get the wrong answer.

Many in Germany assumed the return to prosperity would come from the strong leadership of Adolph Hitler. Not all Germans fell for Hitler's promise of a great revival of the Germanic people and a return to prosperity. The problem was that after Hitler coerced enough votes to get the top job, he was successful at launching a dictatorship with world dominance in mind. Those Germans who saw through him were rapidly eliminated.

Hitler had control of a nation that rejected the true God. Hitler himself would retain that position. So as an enemy of God, what would one of your priorities be? The priority of Hitler's Nazi party, like that of Satan, was the elimination of God's chosen people: the Holocaust, the eradication of six million Jews. The devil was making a move!

Fortunately, not all nations chose the route of tyranny. Back here in the United States and in other countries such as England, the hard times of the Depression resulted in people turning to prayer. Out of poverty and pain, the people saw the error of their ways and returned to faith and prayer. It was a lesson hard learned.

God heard those prayers, and just as he had done so many times with the ancient Israelites, he responded and presented us with a way out. If we had not repented as a nation, who knows what would have happened?

So once again, we became a nation of Christian values. We reclaimed our morality and sense of honesty. A hard day of work would mean dinner on the table. Waste was not tolerated, and we thanked God for our daily blessings. As this generation aged, they were sometimes looked on as being a bit thrifty, but they were just living what they learned, that all one has could vanish in an instant. They knew the value of hard work because they had to work a little harder. Most important of all, they understood biblical principles.

The generation who lived through the Great Depression would be given a huge test of their values and morality when Satan launched his next offensive. If there was ever an earthbound war symbolic of the eternal struggle between good and evil, its name was World War II. Satan selected and groomed some of his favorite heroes to general his onslaught. Names like Hirohito, Mussolini, Hitler, Himmler, Goering, Speer, and Goebbels led a list of earthbound followers of the devil.

The good chess player that he is, Satan was preparing additional moves down the line. He masked as an ally of his enemy a chap called Joseph Stalin, who would murder as many as, and maybe more than, all the axis forces of World War II combined.

The big similarity between Stalin's Communist regime and Hitler's fascist regime was that neither had room for religious faith. The Jew and the Christian were high on the extermination chart. Anyone who had no religion could be brainwashed and of some use to the government. God would prevent total control of the people, so the government had to become God.

It took the attack at Pearl Harbor to finally push the United States into the conflict, but we came together as one nation, undivided, under God. The devil's armies would be defeated with the United States spearheading the charge. With the great victory over evil, America would be blessed with a time of prosperity not previously experienced in human history.

The 1950s in America, while probably sometimes idealized, were, by all historic evidence, a time of Bible-based conservative ethics. America was a Christian nation where all had the right to choose their faith without need to justify their belief, no matter what that may have been. Of course, there were instances of anger and injustice, but there is no such place as utopia, with the single exception of heaven. Where man reigns, there is hatred and wrongdoing. But if that place is believing in Christ, there is always the guidance of the Spirit to help with the constant need for course correction.

So while America was thriving with the blessing of freedom and prosperity that God provided, our earthly adversary remained the same. Old Joe Stalin was out there being used as Satan's puppet. Our archrival was the godless Communist Soviet Union. The same old devil was still up to his silly tricks. But his tricks weren't and still aren't just for kids.

While Satan used the Soviet Union to threaten the United States openly from the front porch, this was only a decoy to draw us from the back door. Undercover from the frontal assault by the Russians, the devil masked his behind-the-scenes efforts to infiltrate and destroy from within. As the United States worried about Communist Russia, we made a determined effort to build up our earthly arsenal. Unfortunately, on a parallel path, we allowed our spiritual arsenal to become depleted.

The United States was still on the straight and narrow entering the 1960s. Under President Kennedy, we didn't flinch at the aggressive movement of Communism into various locales worldwide. The United States stood tall and helped whenever possible to fend off the tyrannical, godless form of government.

In October 1961, when Communist Vietcong guerrillas were repeatedly attacking the government of South Vietnam, Kennedy sent his military adviser, General Maxwell D. Taylor to assist the South. Then on December 11, 1961, the first direct US military assistance was sent to Vietnam. Years after the first American military deployment to Vietnam, it is largely forgotten that it was a noble lending of assistance to a people threatened by a hostile regime. Five months following the assignment of troops to Vietnam, on May 12, 1962, Kennedy responded to Communist forces attempting a violent takeover of Northern Laos by sending naval and ground forces to that country. A little over a month later, something occurred that sent the United States off the path of righteousness.

On June 25, 1962, the United States of America made a conscious decision to make the rejection of God the law of the land. On this date, the Supreme Court of the United States voted to ban any and all prayer in public schools, even if the prayer is denomination-neutral. But that wasn't enough. The ban included any hint of prayer, even if the student chose silence, or if the student was allowed to be excused from the classroom. No prayer, period!

In 1963, the anti-God movement went further and focused on the Christian. On June 17 of that year, the Supreme Court decided there would be no sanctioned Bible study or reading in public schools. No mention was made of the Muslim Koran, the Buddhist Tipitaka, or any other book. Apparently, the Supreme Court felt it was fine to educate oneself and for public schools to educate a student of any subject or belief system as long as Jesus Christ, the Savior of all mankind, was not part of it.

Only the Bible was targeted out of the tens of millions of books ever written. Is this not a clue to the reality of God and the devil? Only one book. Only one deity. Only one teaching. Of the huge number of books, gods, and beliefs, only the book of teaching of one God is singled out. Satan is only interested in attacking the one true God, and he will gladly promote every other false god to steer us astray of the truth. You see, Satan fully understands that once we read and accept the power of the only real Lord and Savior, the devil will have lost us.

Is it possible that just an overactive imagination recognizes this as the point America fell off the cliff? Unaltered history would suggest not. Prior to the ban on Jesus, the United States had never lost a war and always seemed to be on the side opposed to oppression. We had certainly had economic downturns other than the Great Depression, but they were mostly short-lived, and the recovery would usually result in greater prosperity. Our morals were pretty consistently biblical. Absolutely, our country endured periods of Christian apathy, but we always got a handle on it before total disaster happened. We would eventually see the error of our ways and get back on the path to Christ. Christian revivals came in time to save the nation.

Post-World War II America was a nation blessed with abundant riches and freedom. But we wanted more. We wanted the freedom to choose our own God, and if we had to make one up, so be it.

Satan was whispering into ears, planting the seeds of greed and arrogance. Just as we had done in the past, we listened to the lies. We continued the tradition Adam and Eve started. All we needed to do was come back to God, recognizing our sin and repenting from the heart. We could have put a stop to the fall of America, but Christians of the time chose to bury their heads in the sand and hope God would come through. God was waiting for us to act on his will. For the most part, however, Christians sat back and watched as the devil energized his forces to act on his behalf. Tiny, insignificant numbers of nonbelievers would slowly but surely succeed at forcing their views down the throats of the masses. God's earthly followers did nothing as age-honored biblical values were toppled one at a time. It all began with Satan's first great victory at the battle of prayer in schools.

The children of that day became the leaders who despise the Bible. Those kids' parents could have taught them the truth at home, but the indoctrination of the school system proved too strong. It wasn't overwhelming, but it was still too strong for parents with their heads in the sand to combat it. Yes, we blew it, and if I had been there, I might have become just as lazy in my faith as those good folks. The devil is always more than any of us can handle when we have not the aid of God. When we place the Bible in a corner to gather dust, we take the off ramp to the town of biblical ignorance: Mayor Satan, population hell bound.

While Christians did little, the sexual revolution exploded. Sex was the name of the game, and traditional marriage was getting pushed out. It took time, decades to be sure, but traditional marriage finally became something the nonbeliever could shun. Despite God's teaching, homosexual marriage is now the law of the land, and any-one who believes in the laws of marriage as God presents them in the Bible is considered homophobic. Funny that the homosexual who plainly announces hatred of Christians is not considered a Christian-phobe. Again, it should be obvious to the true believer of the presence of the devil in the now-common occurrence of Christian phobia.

By 2016, the growth of anti-Christian sentiment in the United States reached such extremes that it resulted in the arrest of Christian public officials, the closing of Christian-owned businesses, and the firing of Christian employees, all in the name of diversity and polit-ical correctness—for all except the Christian. But, as it turned out, this was only the visible surface of the iceberg. In 2006, the Internal

Revenue Service appointed a woman by the name of Lois Lerner as the director of tax-exempt organizations. At one time, this woman had also been the president of the Council on Government Ethics Laws. She is a lawyer and is married to a tax lawyer. Her knowledge of the law and her concern of governmental ethics would seem above reproach. Not so.

Mrs. Lerner was caught using her authority with the IRS to delay and deny the tax-exempt status of conservative and Christian faith-based organizations due to her political leaning.[20] She claimed a group of IRS employees in Cincinnati, Ohio, were to blame. In May 2013, Lerner was placed on administrative leave, and one year later, she was declared in contempt of Congress. All but six Democrats stuck by her side to the very end.

The year 2018 kicked off with a wave of hatred toward President Trump so vile that all supporters of anything Christian, including Trump himself, would be physically threatened by the anti-God left. Even innocent babies would not be excluded from this hell-inspired hatred.

When Trump won the office of president in 2016, liberals blew up in rage. College students somehow thought burning their own campuses was the appropriate way to express their hatred for the president and our country. So-called comedians found humor in carrying a replica of the severed head of Trump. Laughing like Satan, they didn't see themselves resembling ISIS terrorists doing the same with the actual heads of Christians.

The mainstream media refuses to report the horrors of overseas persecution of Christians and Jews. They will not report the mass beheadings, the mass drownings, the crucifixions, and the burning alive of people for being supporters of Christ and Israel. Instead, American media elects to side with the terrorists for no other reason than Trump and the Bible thumpers oppose the terrorists, who are listening to the advice of Satan. If these horrors become known among the American people, the people might see the error of their ways and support the Christian leader in a Christian nation. But then, death is nothing the devil frowns upon.

On January 29, 2018, United States governing authorities in Washington, DC, spearheaded by the Democrats, voted down the "Pain Capable Unborn Child Protection Act." When medical evidence overwhelmingly proves that at twenty weeks a baby feels pain, why in God's name would anyone choose to continue the barbaric and cruel act of abortion? God's name was not involved; that's why. Cattle and hogs are butchered in a more humane manner than human babies.

In Section 2 of the Act referred to as HR 1797, the legislative findings as declared by Congress determined that at twenty weeks, all pain receptors are present throughout the body and are linked to the brain. At eight weeks, the unborn child reacts to touch. Application of pain stimuli results in an increase of stress hormones.[21]

These infants scream and retreat from the abortionists' tools. Yet, when Heidi Heitkamp, the self-acclaimed Catholic Senator from North Dakota, voted to continue the slaughter, Senate Minority Leader Chuck Schumer of New York congratulated her with a smiling high-five. These two Democratic Party members were overwhelmed with joy at the defeat of a proposal from the right. The celebrations of Satan and his demons was almost audible. Trump and his Christians had been defeated. To hell with the babies. After all, in the womb, nobody can hear a baby scream.

When President Trump nominated Brett Cavanaugh to the Supreme Court of the United States, Judge Kavanaugh was immediately scorned by the left for one reason and one reason only: Kavanaugh happens to believe in the truth of Jesus Christ. At Kavanaugh's confirmation hearing, nearly every Democrat attacked him, but Bernie Sanders exhibited a singular rage so hostile as to be an open declaration of war on all Christianity. Sanders's line of questioning presented the world with more than just a bit of evidence as to his idea of Christianity. His anger was so predominant that it appeared blood would soon pour from his eyes and ears. At any moment, he seemed ready to pull out a gun and point it at Kavanaugh's head. No one on the left saw it. In fact, they hatched another scheme to defeat this Bible nut.

Out of the woodwork came that old Democrat standby. Not racism this time, but sexism. Two women accused Kavanaugh of everything but being Jack the Ripper. One of them quickly recanted her story, admitting it to be a lie, while the other stuck it out. To her own embarrassment, she was proven to be a liar as well. The media played these stories big until the efforts failed. Then the media ignored these two unsuccessful attempts to drag Kavanaugh to his crucifixion, preferring instead to allow the gullible public to wallow in the lie.

While most people assaulting the Bible today are declared members of the one particular political party, by no means are they the only guilty perpetrators. Unbelievers and the deceived populate many organizations and political affiliations. It is not a political party we as Bible believers should fear but the one who designs his sights on devouring that party and all others as well. It is Satan's hope to control our systems of governing, but to accomplish this, he needs to sway enough of the commoners to his side.

Remember the Plebeians of Jesus's day? The regular folk who sided with the leadership to crucify Jesus? Satan is constantly in attack mode, and he has been attempting to conquer the United States since its birth. And now Satan is ready to move on to the final stage of his plan to take down the United States. He has had a ringer lingering on the sidelines since the 1890s, possibly even earlier. That secret weapon is a form of government that calls for the elimination of religious faith.

The presidential election of 1892 was the first in which a Socialist ran for the top job in America. Simon Wing represented the Socialist Labor Party and finished last in a five-man race. But a candidate from the "People's party" came in third. James Weaver took home over a million votes and twenty-two electoral votes representing a party that called for the governmental control of the railroads, restricting growth and influence of corporations, and eliminating the disparity of wealth. In other words, they were attempting through subterfuge to wipe out free trade and capitalism in order to bring on a form of Communism. Communism, like Socialism, allows for a god, but that god is the state.

The People's party largely went away by 1896 when most of the nation saw through their veil. They did manage to put a candidate in the 1904 presidential election, but Thomas E. Watson finished a distant fifth. That same year, Socialist Eugene Debs came in third after a fourth-place finish in 1900. Mr. Debs continued to represent the Socialists on the ballot in 1908 and 1912. He was replaced in 1916 by A. L. Benson but returned in 1920.

With the exception of 1924, there was a Socialist on the presidential ballot every four years until 1952 when the Socialists began to go a different route. The nation had become so blessed that the devil needed to formulate a new strategy. His new scheme would be patience. Keep the Socialist agenda alive on the back-burner while waiting for the next great fall from grace. That fall began in 1962 with the discarding of prayer. But Satan would need diligence in his patience. There was still resistance to the antibiblical agenda and a righteous struggle for civil rights. Time and sneaky persistence would be his allies.

It took Satan over forty years to wrestle control of one of the two major political parties and to intimidate the other until it backed into a corner, offering up nothing more than a token, feeble resistance. The devil is standing so clearly in charge of the left that the people he has deceived now believe in his every utterance. He no longer needs to creep in the shadows, whispering in their ears. He now stands proud with shoulders back and chest out. He has taken command of the left. The old God-fearing, patriotic Democratic Party is gone. But it can be resurrected if the entire nation does not fall first.

The enemies of Satan have their work cut out for them, however. As of 2018, a majority of Democrats are in support of that old godless Socialism. They don't outwardly call it Socialism, but that is part of the deception. The devil's patience and persistence are paying off. America is on the brink of destruction.

Whether a self-proclaiming Christian subscribes to the Democratic or the Republican platform, he or she should still recognize the tools of the devil. Socialism is a stepping stone to Communism, and the only permissible god in a Communist regime is the state.

Godless liberalism is fully integrated into our school system. History is being altered to fit the devil's agenda. God-fearing Christians of the past are now being disestablished. American history is being tilted to provide a fictionalized vision where American biblical values were in reality villainous. The fact that biblical values are being treated as wrong should enlighten the reader to the source of the teaching. The parents of students being brainwashed by the devil's volunteers had better become involved before it is too late.

All biblical teaching is banned from public schools. Creationism is not even permitted as an option or even as a lesson in open-mindedness. The minds of our public school boards are locked shut. Parents need even to be wary of Christian schools, as some of these have been infiltrated by closed minds from the left. Even the vast majority of our colleges and universities that claim to be institutes of higher education and the place to go to learn to open one's mind have degenerated into liberal indoctrination centers.

Satan is using the sins of a few to bring down the many. Remember, sin destroys not only the individual but the entire creation. The great flood of Noah cleansed the whole ball of wax. The tower of Babel, on the other hand, symbolized man claiming equal heights with the Creator. The whole shebang needed an adjustment.

The United States has needed revival in the past and will again. The only question is, will we revive every time we fall? Through the sin of a very small number of people, the entire nation has slid down to the depths of total corruption and lawlessness. God made us male and female, not LGBTQ.

The evidence of the devil and his triumphant effort in swaying the left to his side surrounds us but seems only visible to those of us in the light.

When groups of people cheer the violence against police officers, and this cheer is only derided by one political group, it is yet another sign of spiritual warfare. When one political group that stands on the side of chaos, supporting the "civil rights" of the criminal as a form of opposition to the political group that stands for law and order, there is a problem. When one hates a political party so much that it prompts the person to praise criminal behavior, this is a clear indication of a person rejecting God. It just happens that in the early twenty-first century, one American political party runs campaigns supporting police and law enforcement. This is the same party supported by most evangelical students of God's word.

Unfortunately, it is the party the evangelicals support that has been bullied by Satan into wormlike fortitude. This is why the evangelical believers in the way of Christ are working to dismantle and reassemble the Republican Party. One completely godless party is already too much. That godless party is the one that stands defiant to biblical marriage, life, the two genders, Israel, creationism, Bibles in school and the workplace, and Jesus as the only way to salvation. Now they also reject the people who choose to risk their lives to provide the public with a measure of safety. They turn away from all this for no other reason than the other party supports these things.

That other party became corrupt with cowardice and is now going through bitter hard-fought change. In fact, as an answer to the prayers of the righteous, the party of cowards is being replaced by a party of believers. And the other side is going bananas.

Since the elimination of prayer in the 1960s, it appears the devil has taken control of the left. In response, God is now taking over the right. The Democrats are gone. The Republicans are disappearing. We no longer vote left or right, liberal or conservative, Democrat or Republican. We now choose evil or good. The choice is up to us. We can save ourselves and, at the same time, save our country for future generations, or we can deny ourselves the grace of God and doom the world for today's children.

The two-party system in America is now, and always has been, a good way to thrash out our differences. We need opposing opinions to enable open thinking. The two-party system in the cosmos is now, and always has been, evil trying to take down the good of God's creation. In the end, the one kingdom will win.

When the angels revolted against their Creator, they began a war they could not win. When we, through the freedom God gave us, choose to rebel against our Creator, we begin something we cannot finish. But God loves us so much that he became one with his creation in order to convince us to come back to him.

> For God so loved the world that He gave his one and only son, that whoever believes in Him shall not perish but have eternal life. For God did not send his Son into the world to condemn the world, but to save the world through Him. Whoever believes in Him is not condemned, but whoever does not believe stands condemned already because they have not believed in the name of God's one and only Son. This is the verdict: Light has come into the world, but people loved darkness instead of light because their deeds were evil. Everyone who does evil hates the light, and will not come into the light for fear that their deeds will be exposed. But whoever lives by the truth comes into the light, so that it may be seen plainly that what they have done has been done in the sight of God. (John 3:16–21 NIV)

We were created in his image to love him and each other as we love him. Needless to say, we are getting a failing grade. But God is willing to give us something we do not deserve, something the angels of rebellion are not getting: the gift of eternal salvation with him.

Jesus is the gift. He paid our sin debt for us. He directs us out of the darkness and into the light. Once in the light, we can see the darkness we came from, but those who stay in darkness cannot see the light. If we decline the gift, we remain in the dark. We must accept the gift and open the word in order to grow in maturity, not only for our own sake, but for the sake of others so that the Lord may use us to offer others the same salvation we have received.

If we will only accept the gift and then grow in it.

CHAPTER 11

The Bible, Our Source

So you are interested in discovering the source of all understanding, the light of truth, so you can discern the correct biblical view a Christian should possess. It is time to open God's word for yourself to see what Jesus teaches. Do you wonder if these people who talk about all this good news really have it down pat?

The Bible is such a big book that it seems a daunting task to learn everything in it. So where do we start? The Bible does not need to be read in order from front to back. While doing so can provide a historical timeline, it is not necessary to start reading from "In the beginning" and end at "Amen."

Our current covenant with God begins with the book of Matthew; most church leaders, biblical scholars, and even those of us who have been Christians for a long time, recommend that a new believer begin with the New Testament. Some recommend the gospel of John as a first reading, then the rest of the gospels, and on to the remainder of the New Testament.

I personally feel a newly born Christian start with the four gospels. Any order works, but read all four completely. Continue on to the book of Acts and then Romans. At this point, if you wish to reread the Gospels, that's fine, or you could move into the rest of the New Testament. Let the Spirit in you be your guide.

While the Old Testament provides answers and insights from God, new believers may recognize these answers more easily if they have read the New Testament first. Some of the Old Testament is applicable today and some is not, and what is not necessarily applicable today can influence your understanding of what is of use today. The God of the Old Testament is the same God of the New Testament. The entire Bible is inspired by God and is therefore useful.

After one gains an understanding of who Jesus is today, an understanding of who Jesus was yesterday will follow. You see, the Old Testament is filled with Jesus. But you probably won't recognize him there until you recognize him in our contemporary world. He is all around us, and you will get a better grasp of this through His word in the New Testament.

As you are reading, if there is something you don't understand, don't worry. You will. Take my word, and the word of any other who has read the Bible, you will. (Notice, I said *reader*, not *scholar*.) God's word is meant for everyone, not just supereducated Bible scholars and graduates of Bible school. Any pastor, priest, or minister worth his or her weight in cardboard will be the first to agree that each of us is to form a personal relationship with Jesus, and the word of God speaks to each of us as individuals. This does not mean we have the right to create our own doctrine through misunderstanding of the word, but we are to try to discern the true doctrine as taught by God.

The seminary graduate is here to help guide us on our path, but that same graduate is still human and capable of being deceived by Satan. Someone who dedicates their life to teaching God's word is of great need, but God requires us all to learn, discern, and spread the truth as individuals. God has a different use for each of us.

The Protestant Bible is comprised of sixty-six books. Most are not the length of a single chapter in other books, probably because quite a few were actually letters. So don't be daunted by the idea of reading sixty-six books. Some are as short as a single page. The length of one of these books has no bearing on its ability to change lives. Remember, these are the inspired words of the Creator of the universe.

When you open your Bible, you will find it broken into two parts: the Old Testament and the New Testament. As I have already stated, you want to start in the New Testament. It is the agreement with God that we live by today. But you will read the Old Testament later on.

The books of the Bible are arranged in the following order:

The Old Testament

The Old Testament begins with the five books of Moses: Genesis, Exodus, Leviticus, Numbers, and Deuteronomy. These are also known as the books of the Law. In these books, you will find the account of creation and the early covenants between God and that creation. Some of the more well-known stories that appear in these books are the account of Noah's Ark, the tower of Babel, and the parting of the Red Sea.

Next you will find a group of books that include a bit of everything. They are Joshua, Judges, Ruth, 1 and 2 Samuel, 1 and 2 Kings, 1 and 2 Chronicles, Esther, Nehemiah, Job, Psalms, Proverbs, Ecclesiastes, and the Song of Solomon. These books pick up the history where the first five left off. They are referred to as the poetic books, which include many famous and worthwhile sayings you will be quite surprised come from the Bible. Some prophecy is witnessed as well.

The final portion of the Old Testament provides additional historic info and the majority of prophecy. These books include Isaiah, Jeremiah, Lamentations, Ezekiel, Daniel, Hosea, Joel, Amos, Obadiah, Jonah, Micah, Nahum, Habakkuk, Zephaniah, and Malachi.

The prophets were exactly what the word means. The prophecies found in the Bible are nothing like the alleged "prophecies" of Nostradamus or any other so-called prophet or mind-reader whose sayings are so vague that they can be construed in any sort of way. These guys in the Bible were the real deal. The prophecies these folks claimed, all of which came true 100 percent, were made well in advance of when the events in the prophecies actually happened, and were detailed with extreme accuracy. This stuff is supernatural.

They prophesied the coming Messiah between 500 and 1,400 years prior to his arrival with such accuracy that it would give you a headache. But don't be tempted to go straight to these books. To understand, you will need to know the prophecies fulfilled first. These are revealed in the New Testament.

This stuff is awesome, and when you understand, the evidence for proving the reality of God and Satan is as convincing as it gets.

The New Testament

The New Testament opens with Matthew, Mark, Luke, and John, collectively referred to as "the Gospels," which actually means "good news." What good news? The good news that the Messiah, the Savior, has arrived. The first four books of the New Testament are the story of God in human form, the story and teachings of Jesus. Christ is not his last name, however. He is the Christ. He is the Messiah. He is the Savior.

The fifth book of the New Testament was written by Luke, the same author of the gospel by this name. Many scholars consider it a continuation of the gospel story, sort of a fifth gospel. It is a historical sequel to the four gospels.

Acts tells the story of what happened immediately following Christ's crucifixion. In this book, we learn the price of faith, the joy and the struggle of what it means to be a believer. This is the story of the first believers, the ones who knew Jesus firsthand. Here we learn of the persecution they were willing to take because of their faith. These are the people who cowered and hid after Jesus was crucified but three days later were willing to be tortured and die rather than reject the Savior. Nobody dies for a lie. Jesus did rise.

The next group of books were letters written to individuals or churches, and they were composed to instruct and inspire. They are Romans; 1 and 2 Corinthians; Galatians; Ephesians; Philippians; Colossians; 1 and 2 Thessalonians; 1 and 2 Timothy; Titus; Philemon; Hebrews; James; 1, 2 and 3 John; and Jude.

These letters were not only directed at the contemporary reader of that time but to all people from any time. Daily we need to be refreshed with God's word. The Bible is the only book we can read a thousand times and still get new revelation. These letters, which God gave to all of us, are the most informative and helpful letters we will ever receive.

The final book, the book of Revelation, is another book of prophecy. While the Old Testament prophets told of Jesus's first coming, they also spoke of his second coming. This final book can only be understood when we understand how the New Testament works with the Old Testament. Its meaning is revealed in the combining of the testaments. This is truly a book for the enlightened in Christ. In these words, we can learn and see the truth of the great Creator. It is no coincidence that those who don't believe see nothing.

The unsaved usually consider the last book of the Bible the ramblings of a madman, or simply a drug-induced hallucination. They see nothing, for they lack the presence of the Holy Spirit. They mock the believer, exactly as Jesus said they would.

If you claim to be Christian, and you wish to vote biblically, you must step out of darkness. You must be enlightened to receive the revelation of the Lord. If you pray and open your Bible, the only source of truth, this blessing can be yours. The only way to light the way of escape from the temptation and lies of Satan is by knowing and growing in the understanding of God's word.

If you claim Christianity as your faith, it is essential that you follow God's command to tell others. If you won't even read the Bible to enhance your own knowledge, how can your Savior use you to save others? Or are you concerned only about your own salvation? Many are unaware that there are Jews who read and understand the Bible better than most Christians. These are the Messianic Jews. These are the Jews of the Old and New Covenants. These are Jews who read and, more importantly, believe Old Testament prophecy, which told of the coming Savior, the coming Messiah. The Messiah is the Savior, and Jesus met the full criteria.

We must not forget that Jesus was a Jew who went to temple and adhered to Jewish customs. All the first believers in Jesus as Savior were Jews. Today, these Jews are known as messianic because they accepted the teachings of the Old Testament to obey the teachings of the New Testament. Yes, these contemporary Jews study the Bible with more fervor than most self-proclaiming Christians, who could learn a boatload from the Messianic Jews about what they perceive as their own religion.

Are you starting to comprehend the connection between the Testaments? If you open your Bible, you will not only grow in knowledge, but you will also grow in love and inspiration. A true born-again Christian, destined for eternity with Jesus, after tasting his word, will hunger for more and will feel the need to share it.

Do not be afraid. Wanting to spread the word does not mean approaching strangers or knocking on doors. God will lead you, and many times, he will actually send some to you with questions that God knows you have the ability to answer. While you may feel frightened to respond to the questions, there is no basis for this apprehension. The devil wants you to fear. He needs you to chicken out, for if you do, then the person with the question will not hear the word of Christ. The devil wants all of us to be apprehensive and unsure of ourselves. Satan wants us to be insecure about our ability to respond with answers.

Satan is correct about one thing: we are all unable to respond correctly, but only if we put our faith in our own knowledge. When we rely solely on our own capabilities, defeat is imminent. All we need to do is remember that we have a ringer on our team. When we recall that the Spirit of God who resides inside us will be fighting our battles, it is easy to answer almost any query. All we have to do is allow ourselves to grow in the word, and God will answer any question through us.

There is nothing to fear. God has blessed us with different talents and desires. We all have strengths unique to us as individuals, and the Lord knows these skills better than we do. If someone asks you a question regarding Christian values or the Christian faith, it is because God directed that individual to you. God knows what the person needs to hear. You may hem and haw and adlib an answer, and that's cool. God knew that's what the person needed to hear, and how he or she needed to hear it. God may also want you to learn the answer and get back to the person, in effect teaching you as well as the inquisitor.

We all need to keep in mind that God's plan for us is something we cannot know. If you are trying to answer a question using your biblical knowledge, you can't be doing a bad thing. If you immerse yourself in the truth, God will be greater served by you. We all experience fear of failure. We all struggle with self-doubt at some time. Even the people of the Bible were just that: people. Moses was no different than many of us today. He was scared to death to take on Pharaoh. He shook with fear and apprehension and came up with every excuse under the sun why he was not suitable for God to use him. But God knew him better than he knew himself.

Moses eventually obeyed God and stood up to Pharaoh. God kept His promise then, just like he does today. He was right there with Moses, and he will be right here with us when we obey. Exactly as Moses and every other Christian, we will probably take some heat for our faith, but the rewards coming from obedience will be out of this world. The other side will rise in hatred, but when the power of the Almighty Creator is in your corner, you cannot lose. Sometimes, your situation will seem bleak, but victory is at hand.

When you have the courage to select righteous leadership, you display the strength of Jesus to overcome evil. You allow God to use you to put in place an earthly government dedicated to defeating evil.

Before you can do this simple thing for good, however, you need to see clearly the ways of Satan and the ways of Jesus. As God is outside time as we know it, this book, being inspired by the Holy Spirit living within, shall end where it began.

Political issues can and will always be divisive because politics reflect the thinking of man. No matter how well-intentioned, the plans of man are always flawed because man is not all-knowing. Only one is all-knowing, and he ain't no man. To hone your skills so God can better use you, read his words. Learn his way. Open the source.

Good reading!

Special thank you to Frank for presenting me with my first bible three decades ago. Thank you to Donna Ferrier out in Oklahoma. "It isn't April 1 yet." Your skills as a Christian editor are unmatched and your faith and dedication are a blessing. I'm happy I found you in the nick of time. Thank you to Shawn Cornett and Ron York in Indiana. Your sermons and teaching are more valuable than you know.

SOURCES

This work was primarily inspired by God's word as presented in the Holy Bible. External sources of information came from the following list. No exact quotes were used. No part of any of these sources was reproduced in any way, other than the title, publisher, and date of copyright.

Ancient Biblical History

A Visual Walk Through Genesis. © 2016 Stephen M. Miller, published by Harvest House Publishers.

Encyclopedia Britannica 1956. Copyright under International Copyright Union by Encyclopedia Britannica.

Smith's Bible Dictionary. © 1986 by Thomas Nelson, Inc.

The Complete People & Places of the Bible, Pamela L. McQuade. © 2014 by Barbour Publishing Inc.

The Essential Bible Reference Library. © 1998 The Moody Bible Institute of Chicago.

The Handy History Answer Book. © 1999 by Visible Ink Press.

The Lion Concise Atlas of Bible History. Original text by Paul Lawrence. This concise edition edited by Richard Johnson. This edition © 2012 by Lion Hudson.

Post Biblical and Contemporary History

Encyclopaedia Britannica
    1956 Copyright under International Copyright Union by Encyclopaedia Britannica.

Lincoln's Thought And The Present.
   By Geoffrey C. Ward
   © Copyright 1978, Sangamon State University
PRESIDENTS
ALL YOU NEED TO KNOW
   Hylas Publishing®
   Text Copyright: Hylas Publishing 2004, 2005
The American Patriots Bible
   Copyright © 2009 by Thomas Nelson, Inc.
   Notes and Articles © 2009 by Richard G. Lee
The Founders Bible
   Copyright © 2012 by Shiloh Road Publishers, LLC
   Signature Historian DAVID BARTON
   Brad Cummings & Lance Wubbels, General Editors
National Archives and Records Administration
   Via National Archives webprogram@nara.gov

Doctrine and Philosophy Helps

Awakening To Messiah
   Copyright © 2010 Messianic Rabi K.A. Schneider
   WestBow Press rev. date: 10/14/2010
BELIEVE THIS NOT THAT, ABOUT GOD
   A promise from Heaven for Enery Need on Earth
   Copyright © 2014 by Inprov, Ltd.
Christian Phlosophy
   by Andrew Wommack
   Copyright © 2012 by Andrew Wommack
   Published by Harrison House Publishers, Inc.
Critical Spirit: Confronting the Heart of a Critic
   Copyright © 2015 Hope For The Heart
   June Hunt
   Aspire Press, an imprint of Rose Publishing, Inc.

Keys To Avoiding Deception
  Keys for Living
  Huntley Brown
  Huntley Brown Ministries
  Copyright © 2017

Additional Sources of Background Information

Deluxe Then and Now Bible Maps
  Copyright © 2008 RW Research, Inc.
  All rights reserved.
  Rose Publishing, Inc.
  4733 Torrance Blvd., #259
  Torrance, California 90503 USA
  www.rose-publishing.com
Guttmacher Institute
  listadmin@guttmacher.org
National Archives and Records Administration
  via National Archives webprogram@nara.gov
Strong's Exhaustive Concordance of the Bible:
  Updated and Expanded Edition
  © 2007 Hendrickson Publishers, Inc. P.O. Box 3473
  Peabody, Massachusetts 01961-3473

Chapter Notes

Chapter One

1. 2. 3. 4. 5. 6. Abortions Info-The truth about abortions for all.
Abortion-Without the rhetoric.
https:abortion.info/politics/president-and-abortion/billclinton
accessed 1-20-2019

Chapter Two

7. Chicago Tribune
JULY 25, 2012, 12:01 AM
Alderman to Chic-fil-A: No deal
By Hal Dardick, Chicago Tribune reporter.
https://www.chicagotribune.com/buisness/ct

Chapter Three

8. New York Times
Take a number
37.2 trillion: Galaxies or Human cells?
By Nicholas Bakalar
6-19-15

Chapter Five

9. Reasons U.S. Women Have Abortions;
Quantitative and Qualitive Perspectives

By Lawrence B. Finer, Lori F. Frohwirth, Lindsay A. Dauphinee, Susheela Singh and Ann M. Moore. All at the Guttmacher Institute, New York. September 2005

10. 11. *Christian Philosophy*
by Andrew Wommack
Copyright©2012 by Andrew Wommack
Published by Harrison House Publishers, Inc.

Chapter Eight

12. Library of Congress-Information Bulletin-June 1998—Vol. 57, No 6
Jefferson's Letter to the Danbury Baptists
THE Final Letter, as Sent
13. "I've noticed that everybody that is for abortion has already been born."
Reagan-Anderson Presidential Debate
Baltimore, Maryland
September 21, 1980

Chapter Nine

14. OBERGEFELL ET AL. V. HODGES,DIRECTOR, ET AL
CERTIORARI TO THE UNITED STATES COURT OF APPEALS FOR THE SIXTH CIRCUIT
No. 14–556. Argued April 28, 2015—Decided June 26, 2015
15. *NEWSWEEK*
WHO IS JACK PHILLIPS?
MEET THE CHRISTIAN BAKER IN THE MASTER-PIECE CAKESHOP SUPREME COURT CASE
BY LINLEY SANDERS ON 12/5/17 AT 9:04 AM
16. ALLIANCE DEFENDING FREEDOM
MASTERPIECE CAKESHOP V. COLORADO CIVIL RIGHTS COMMISION
https://www.adflegal.org/detailspages/case-details/
masterpiece-cakeshop-v.-craig
accesed 1/23/2019

Chapter Ten

17. *Forced into Glory: Abraham Lincoln's White Dream*
By Lerone Bennett, Jr.
Chicago; Johnson Publishing Company, 2000
Pp. 652.
18. Sunday State-Journal Register of Springfield, Illinois
June 25, 2000
Great Emancipator or Grand Wizard
Copyright 2000 By Edward Steers Jr.
19. The New York Times
ON THE WEB
August 27, 2000
Lincoln the Devil
Lerone Bennett Jr. is not deceived by the tricks that fooled
Frederick Douglass and Martin Luther King Jr.
By JAMES MCPHERSON
20. FOX NEWS
TAXES
Lois Lerner Got off easy in the IRS scandal. It's time to reexamine the targeting of conservatives.
By Jay Seculow, /Fox news
Jay Sekulow is Chief Counsel of the American Center for Law
and Justice.
21. H.R.1797 (113): Pain Capable Unborn Child Protection Act

About the Author

Thomas W. Paxton was raised as a Catholic and submitted to all the sacraments. He did not, however, study the word of God on his own before the age of thirty-three. A young man of nineteen saw Paxton's ignorance and persisted in guiding him to the truth of God's word. This youthful believer was not seminary trained. He was just out of high school, but he studied with the greatest teacher of all time—the Advocate. This is when Paxton first accepted the gift of grace from our Savior.

At that moment, God began his rebuilding job. Paxton was stripped of anything related to his godless behavior and resurrected as a new creation. Today he possesses the same qualification as that young man who gave him his first Bible some thirty years ago.

While Paxton readily accepts his many flaws, and like all of us, still struggles with temptation from the evil one, he understands that is precisely why we *all* need a Savior.